*The consultancy study was commissioned by the
Forum for Peace and Reconciliation. A first draft was
presented to the Forum at its meeting on 14 July 1995
and was finalized on 29 December 1995. The views
expressed are those of the author and are not necessarily
those of the Forum or its members.
Publication, with an accompanying Forum commentary,
was authorized by the Forum's Coordinating Committee
on 15 December 1995, subject to final clearance by
the Sub-Committee on Fundamental Rights.
In view of the continuing deferral, since early
February 1996, of meetings of the Forum and
of its committees, the study is now being published,
without the commentary, on the authority of the
Chairperson, because of its relevance to the peace
processs and all-party negotiations.
It is hoped to publish the Forum commentary at a later date.*

TABLE OF CONTENTS

EXECUTIVE SUMMARY AND ISSUES OF RELEVANCE

A. PURPOSE AND MANDATE

1. By letter of 6 March 1995, the Forum for Peace and Reconciliation requested me to prepare a study with the following mandate: (a) to present the evolution of international law and international practice in regional organizations concerning guidelines for group accommodation and minority protection in divided societies; (b) to review relevant practices in political systems of selected plural societies; taking into account the constitutional provisions, legal decisions and administrative arrangements; (c) to distil from the above those elements which are of potential value for the discussion of options in the Irish context.

2. A draft was presented in July 1995 and formed the basis of a discussion at the plenary session of the Forum, to which I was invited, on 14 July 1995. While the general approach was widely appreciated by the participants, constructive suggestions were made by representatives of the different parties and groups constituting the Forum. These observations have also been made available to me as transcripts of the discussions. In addition, Sinn Féin have made two useful written submissions.

3. The mandate did not call on me to make recommendations in regard to Northern Ireland, or Ireland as a whole. As stated by the Acting Chairperson of the meeting on 14 July, Senator Jan O'Sullivan, it would be for the members of the Forum to agree on the lessons to be drawn from how other societies handle diversity and division. The benefit of the study would be to see the Irish issues in the international context, including comparisons with other situations, while taking into account that no exact parallels can be drawn.

4.   While abstaining from making specific recommendations, I have been asked to distil from the evolution of international law and practice, and from national experiences in other societies, those elements which are of potential relevance for options in the Irish context. In the body of the study I have therefore not examined the Irish case as such, but in this executive summary I have to make some brief comments on it in order to identify the relevant issues.

B.   OUTLINE OF THE STUDY

5.   The study is divided into six chapters. The first two are mainly conceptual, to set the stage for a more comprehensive exploration in subsequent chapters. Chapter 1 introduces the distinction between territorial disputes and policies inside divided States, and examines in greater detail categories of such policies. It is noted that in many States, contemporary policies aim at integration rather than assimilation. This implies the creation of a common domain, while leaving a more or less comprehensive space to the maintenance of plural identities. Chapter 2 reviews various ways to define group conflicts. Several and quite different forms can be observed under the overall heading of ethnic or religious conflict; it has been shown that different claims are used depending on how the nature of the conflict is perceived. Also, different members of the same group may have different conceptions of the nature of the conflict, and therefore also pursue different claims; this may be due to differences in values and interests. Furthermore, the claims change over time depending, inter alia, on the authorities' response to the assertion of the particular claims. When reasonable and moderate claims are accepted by the authorities or by the dominant side, compromises are worked out making it possible to move forward to a more satisfactory solution in the next step. If, however, even reasonable claims are rejected and/or are met by force, the outcome is likely to be a further polarization and confrontation, leading to the slippery slope to violence.

6.   I turn in chapter 3 to major principles of international law relevant to these issues, focusing particularly on sovereignty, territorial integrity and self-determination. The discussion held on 14 July and subsequent submissions have been of great help in finalizing that chapter. The relationship between territorial integrity and self-determination is a very controversial issue at present. The United Nations has

reviewed the application in practice of the right to self-determination. It has been noted that the post-1945 approach differs significantly from that of the League of Nations. At the peace conferences in 1919-1920 there was wide political support for the principle of national self-determination, but it did not emerge as a general principle of international law. Under United Nations law, self-determination is understood in a territorial rather than an ethnic or national sense, and has been understood to provide a right to independence for non-self-governing territories, and a permanent right to democratic governance for the people of sovereign States. Its relevance for the Irish situation will be touched on below. The chapter also refers briefly to the evolution and content of minority rights as components of contemporary international law, but leaves the fuller discussion of those issues to the following chapter.

7.   Chapter 4 outlines the threefold approach to group accommodation: equality in the common domain, pluralism in togetherness, and territorial subdivision. It provides a review of the development of international standards in these fields, and their implementation in national practice. The principles of equality and non-discrimination guide all modern societies. The section on minority rights explores issues of communal rights, including the debate on collective rights, and outlines elements of accommodation contained in contemporary minority rights instruments, drawing also on examples from national practice. The section on pluralism by territorial subdivision is intended to facilitate a comparison of the rather special case of Northern Ireland with other cases, where autonomy has been a useful instrument in group accommodation, but only when the national minority was a majority within the autonomous area, and thus quite different from the situation in Northern Ireland.

8.   Chapter 5 discusses the interlinkages between the evolution of international law, the evolution of the State system, and of nationalism. It has a dual purpose. One is a somewhat theoretical point: to show that the concept of State and the dual concepts of nation have affected both international law and international relations. There is an important difficulty in discourse when different participants understand the basic notions quite differently; the concept of nation is one to which various meanings are given by different people.

9.   The second part of the chapter deals with somewhat more practical questions: the international legal environment for group accommodation inside States. It explores

3

the utilization of bilateral treaties, an approach extensively used during the League of Nations in the inter-war years, but without much success. It further explores the re-emergence of this notion in the context of the European Stability Pact during the last few years, and notes that the Anglo-Irish Agreement, 1985, the Joint Declaration, 1993, as well as the proposals of the British and Irish Governments as set out in *A New Framework for Agreement,* 1995 (if these or equivalent arrangements were to be agreed) provide exemplary models of ways in which bilateral agreements and co-operation can facilitate the accommodation of groups in divided States. The chapter finally considers the evolution of the role of the Council of Europe, the OSCE, and the United Nations.

10.   Finally, chapter 6 compares national experiences. It is preceded by a brief description of the distinction between State-nation and nation-State, which was introduced in the previous chapter. Following that it examines the dynamics of accommodation in a number of ethnically divided State-nations. It has been shown that in some of them, there have been past periods of severe centralization and enforced assimilation to the dominant culture and language, but that this has in recent times been replaced by compromises, making it possible to develop the concept of society and nationhood on two levels: the State as the common home for all, while separate ethno-national or group identities are respected and promoted. The approaches chosen to achieve this result, including decentralization, power-sharing or weighted voting, and extensive legislation concerning language and education are reviewed.

C.   UNDERLYING PRINCIPLES

11.   The essential principles of the emerging peaceful world order can be found in Article 2 of the United Nations Charter, as further elaborated in the Declaration on the Principles of International Law concerning Friendly Relations and Co-operation among States, contained in General Assembly resolution 2625 (XXV). Seven principles are listed: (a) that States shall refrain from the use of force against the territorial integrity and political independence of other States; (b) that States shall settle their international disputes peacefully; (c) the duty not to intervene in matters within the domestic jurisdiction of States; (d) the duty of States to

cooperate with one another in accordance with the Charter, (e) equal rights and self-determination of peoples; (f) sovereign equality of States; (g) that States shall fulfil in good faith their obligations assumed by them in accordance with the Charter.

12.   The relationship between sovereignty, territorial integrity and self-determination is widely debated at present, and is indeed relevant to the Irish situation; some comments, therefore, will be made below.

13.   Apart from the issue of self-determination, manifestations and implementation of group rights, whether those of the majority or of minorities, must be compatible with the basic requirements of a civic society, which are found in the system of human rights now contained in international law. The rights of such groups and their members to preserve and develop their identity have become a major concern in the United Nations, as evidenced in particular through the United Nations General Assembly's adoption in 1992 of the Declaration on the Rights of Persons belonging to National or Ethnic, Religious and Linguistic Minorities.

14.   Since it is essential for all States to develop a satisfactory social and ethnic contract in society, at least three concerns should be simultaneously pursued by States in their domestic policies: (a) to safeguard and enhance equality between all members in society; (b) yet tolerate and promote group diversity by respecting their separate and preferred identity; (c) and do this in democratic and peaceful ways which consolidate and advance stability, both domestically and internationally. States should be encouraged, assisted and prompted by the international community to pursue these aims, in the search for an increasingly stable, non-violent and legitimate world order. Correspondingly, members of minor or major groups, while asserting their particular and preferred identity, must contribute to the evolution of conditions under which equality in the enjoyment of human rights can be ensured for all, including those who do not belong to these groups, and to the promotion of peace and stability within the nation at large. While the international community should advance the protection of members of groups and enhance their ability to maintain their identity, it should also discourage policies or actions by such groups which by use of violence and non-democratic means challenge equality or undermine the political independence and territorial integrity of the State.

D. EXPLORING ISSUES OF RELEVANCE TO OPTIONS IN THE IRISH CONTEXT

TERRITORIAL INTEGRITY AND SELF-DETERMINATION

15.   This study pays close attention to the right of peoples to self-determination. For reasons of international peace and stability, however, international law as it stands today gives territorial integrity precedence over assertions of rights to secession or change of borders. Exceptions to this precedence for territorial integrity occur in the following circumstances: (a) for non-self-governing territories fulfilling the criteria of identification contained in United Nations General Assembly resolution 1514 (XV), as presented in chapter 3, or (b) in quite exceptional cases, when the population of a part of a State has been subjected to consistent and systematic discrimination and when the government of the State concerned is not representative of that part of the population.

16.   These observations, however, do not exhaust the issue of self-determination. A preference for self-determination can be met by agreement between the parties involved, including express recognition by the authorities concerned. There is clearly no obstacle in principle, under international law, to peaceful change of borders by consent. Peaceful and democratic advocacy of such change conforms fully with international law.

17.   In the case of Ireland, the Joint Declaration of 1993 and the Framework Agreement of 1995 include an express recognition by the British Government of the principle of self-determination, and a declared willingness to accept and support a decision concurrently made by the majorities in each of the two parts of Ireland for the establishment of a united Ireland.

18.   The principle of self-determination, although promoted initially by President Wilson's 14 points Address, came to be recognized as a right under international law only well after World War II, and was accepted as such only with the adoption of the Covenants on Human Rights in 1966. Having emerged as a right of peoples it has been understood to provide a right to separate Statehood only to non-self-governing territories.

19. Sinn Féin argues in its submission that Northern Ireland could be seen as the remaining part of a non-self-governing territory, resulting from the disruption of territory at the time when the Republic of Ireland gained independence. It is generally accepted that the division of Ireland created a somewhat irregular situation, and this is probably why Britain has accepted that the principle of self-determination is applicable in this situation and that a decision concurrently made by the majorities of the two parts of Ireland in favour of a united Ireland will be accepted. Even if Northern Ireland is held to be non-self-governing, it would be for the majority of the population of that territory, in line with the relevant resolutions of the United Nations described in chapter 3, to decide on the future of the territory. Should the majority decide in favour of a united Ireland, they could do so, which amounts to what is envisaged in the Anglo-Irish Agreement, the Joint Declaration and *A New Framework for Agreement*.

20. It has been suggested that an analogy could be drawn from the treatment of colonial enclaves within United Nations practice. If so, it could be argued that Northern Ireland should revert to the Republic of Ireland by a majority decision of the population in the island as a whole. In practice, however, all colonial enclaves have been territories not forming regular parts of the colonial metropolitan area, but territories in a subordinate position defined as non-self-governing territories. The exception made for colonial enclaves as distinct from other colonial territories is that they have not been given the option to emerge as independent States, but have had to accept reincorporation into the surrounding States of which they legally formed a part before colonization. Taking into account the history prior to, and the developments which have taken place since partition, it would in any case be necessary to have the consent of the population living in Northern Ireland.

21. It appears, therefore, that the options are continued union with the United Kingdom or agreement to establish a united Ireland if the two parts of Ireland concurrently and by majority so decide.

22. Whichever option is exercised, steps will hopefully be taken to improve the conditions of peaceful cohabitation in Northern Ireland, expanding North-South cooperation and ensuring to both groups full rights to preserve, on a basis of equality, their identity, traditions and respective preferences for future outcomes. Since there exists a formally recognized option for present and future majorities in Northern Ireland to declare themselves in favour of a united Ireland, there can be no

grounds for prohibition of peaceful and democratic activities seeking to influence the public opinion in favour of such an option. The nationalists' preference must therefore have the same acceptance and legitimacy as that of the unionists. The enactment of parity of esteem or equality of treatment in Northern Ireland implies that an equal right of expression for the constitutional preferences and for the identities of all its inhabitants be legally protected.

23.   The legitimate competing approaches to nationhood must not preclude the development of a civic society in Northern Ireland in which each community can participate on an egalitarian basis. It is fully possible for people to identify, in parallel, with different political or geographical units, without causing intolerable strain on the common civic society. Thus, there is a great number of practical tasks which those living in Northern Ireland must undertake in cooperation, irrespective of their different views on future political arrangements, and which they can tackle together without discarding their differing allegiances, identities or cultural affiliations.

24.   In pursuit of general principles the approach should be to combine parity of esteem for the two traditions with the encouragement, through legal and administrative measures, of the fullest possible cooperation and interaction in all fields and allowing full freedom of movement and residence. It is assumed that any measures leading to further physical separation within Northern Ireland, based on communal identity, should be avoided. The experience in other parts of the world, including Bosnia, of dividing land by ethnic or religious identity, is so frightening that it should be avoided at all costs.

AUTONOMY?

25.   Assuming that Northern Ireland will remain, at least for some time, part of the United Kingdom but unique in the arrangements for its internal government and in its links with the Republic, it would be relevant to reflect on the options for the political structure of that part of Ireland.

26.   In many societies, territorial autonomy has proved useful in defusing tension and accommodating different national groups. A balance can be achieved between majority and minority when the majority in the autonomous area is a minority in the country as a whole. The balance is achieved by a division of power between the centre

and the autonomous area, making it possible for the local majority to offset some of the consequences of the assimilationist or hegemonical tendencies in the centre. It is applicable only where there is a compact settlement of the national minority in that particular territory, not when the minority is dispersed throughout the whole country. Such an arrangement might be relevant to proposals leading to a new agreed Ireland.

27. Examples are given in chapter 6 of such arrangements in several countries: Spain, where they have been particularly successful; the Åland Islands; South Tyrol; and the somewhat different type of decentralization on linguistic grounds which has taken place in Belgium.

28. All of these cases provide useful lessons, but they have one aspect in common which does not apply to the situation in Northern Ireland: the absence, within the autonomous area itself, of a deeply divided society. The Åland Islands are almost completely homogeneous in ethnic terms; in the Basque Province there are no serious conflicts between the Basques proper and the Castilians living in the Basque Province; and the same applies to Catalonia. In all of these areas, autonomy has made it possible for a national group, which constitutes a minority in the country as a whole, to develop and strengthen its culture by its predominant influence in the regional political system.

29. In the particular situation of Northern Ireland, autonomy had the opposite impact. The institutions created in Northern Ireland, by failing to take account of the divided nature of society there, and the subsequent abuse of the majoritarian principle, exacerbated division.

30. Therefore, autonomy in such situations is not in itself a good vehicle for solving group conflicts, unless different structures of political decision-making can be adopted, as discussed in chapter 4, ensuring broad-based democracy and cross-community consensus, not ethnocratic majoritarian rule. This principle should apply whether Northern Ireland remains part of the United Kingdom or if in the future an agreed Ireland is established.

31. A point to be drawn from the comparison of national practices in chapter 4 is the use of gradual transfer of authority. In the case of Spain and its autonomous provinces, as in the case of Denmark in its relations with Greenland, sophisticated

approaches have been chosen by which some powers are immediately transferred, others are reserved for the central authorities, while the third and probably the most important set are subjects of negotiation as to the time and scope of their transfer. In this way it is possible to have a gradualist approach which can be adapted to a demonstrated ability and capability to make constructive use of the authority transferred.

IMPLEMENTATION OF HUMAN RIGHTS AND MINORITY RIGHTS — CONSTITUTIONAL AND LEGISLATIVE MEASURES

32.   Harold Jackson has noted that:

> Within their own enclave the Protestants of Ulster, one million strong, outnumber their Catholic brethren by two to one. But in the wider context of Ireland they themselves are easily outnumbered three to one. The inevitable and disastrous result was the advent of a ruling establishment with the reins of power in its hands but acting under the stresses of a besieged minority.[1]

33.   This situation has created serious human rights problems. Among them have been human rights violations arising from the tension surrounding the advocacy of political change. In light both of the legal history and the future visions contained in the Anglo-Irish Agreement, the Joint Declararation and the Framework for Agreement, it must be clear that expressions of communal identities and national allegiances and aspirations, whether nationalist or unionist, are fully legitimate and that no negative sanctions can be imposed on either side for asserting, democratically and peacefully, their respective preferences.

34.   Assuming that a comprehensive political settlement, as envisaged in the Framework for Agreement, will be negotiated and agreed between the two Governments and the political parties in Northern Ireland, followed by popular endorsement by referendum, it will subsequently be given legal and constitutional form through cooperation between the Parliaments in Dublin and London.

35.   One aspect of the new arrangements would thus be a devolved administration in Northern Ireland based on cross-community consensus. It must further be assumed that Northern Ireland, while linked to the United Kingdom, will have to be treated

as a territory apart in the sense that special regulations will have to be applicable because of the divided composition of its society. This, I submit, would have to be the case also if in the future a majority wished for and consented to the establishment of a united Ireland, in particular if that were to occur not as a consequence of a change in the unionist aspiration but as a result of an altered numerical balance between the two communities. In deeply divided societies it is a widespread practice to include guarantees in constitutional provisions. This can consist of a formal recognition of the existence of the separate groups, coupled with appropriate guarantees to ensure that statutory law and administrative practice comply with respect for the identity and interests of both sides.

36.   It is an increasingly widespread practice to incorporate international human rights law in relevant domestic legislation, in many cases through constitutional provisions. The United Kingdom and the Republic of Ireland are practically the only States members of the Council of Europe which have not incorporated international human rights law into their own constitutions and legal order.

37.   As a minimum, the European Convention on Human Rights and Fundamental Freedom should be incorporated; preferably, incorporation should include also the International Covenants adopted by the United Nations. This could be done specifically for Northern Ireland in a revised Northern Ireland Constitutional Act. It would be desirable that it be done also by the Republic of Ireland and the United Kingdom, in order to ensure harmony of law in respect of universal human rights throughout these societies. Legislative measures should be taken to ensure full implementation of the International Convention on the Elimination of all Forms of Racial Discrimination (ICERD), which also covers ethnic discrimination. It is noted that specific legislation — the Fair Employment (Northern Ireland) Act of 1989 — is already in place; this could be extended to other areas covered by ICERD and other international instruments.

38.   This in itself would not guarantee equal consideration and fair treatment of both traditions; therefore, additional provisions would be required. Several constitutions which explicitly recognize the existence of separate groups and require equality of treatment can offer guidance. An example, where language is used as the relevant criterion, can be found in the Constitution Act of Finland, section 14, which includes the following elements:

Finnish and Swedish are the national languages of the Republic. …

The cultural and economic needs of the Finnish-speaking and Swedish-speaking populations shall be met by the State according to the principle of equality.

(For more details see chapter 6.)

POLITICAL ARRANGEMENTS

39. The notion of power-sharing has often been used in the context of political arrangements in divided societies. It has its problems, and it is not here argued that a formal power-sharing in the executive branch should be imposed. There are interesting models, for instance from South Tyrol, which can be useful. It appears, however, that even better opportunities might exist in the context of the evolving situation concerning Northern Ireland. While a degree of autonomy for the territory may be required, it cannot be fully implemented until it is ensured that equality exists on all levels in that society. Such equality has increased during the years of direct rule but must be consolidated and further improved. This is also generally recognized in the Joint Declaration and the proposals set out in *A New Framework for Agreement.*

40. In divided societies electoral systems could be established which reward compromise over exclusively ethnic voting. This would be facilitated by proportional representation and weighted voting. It may be difficult because it could block decision-making altogether. It is noted that the proposals set out in *A New Framework for Agreement* and by the British Government in relation to accountable government in Northern Ireland appreciate the necessity of mechanisms to cope with stalemate in, or the breakdown of, the new institutions to be created.

41. The following options might therefore be examined:

- Prior to devolution of power, the adoption of a comprehensive set of statutes in accordance with the requirements of international human rights law, ensuring equality in the common domain and the organization of the administration of justice, security forces and others, on a basis of impartiality.

- Power should be devolved only if adequate arrangements are put in place to guarantee the immutability, other than through consensus, of basic requirements regarding proportional representation and weighted voting.

42.   As envisaged in the agreements between the Irish and British Governments that package of laws to be formally adopted by the British Parliament would have to emerge through agreement in all-party talks and would have to receive popular endorsement.

43.   In order for legislation to provide satisfactory guarantees, the composition of the courts must also be taken into account. Guidance can be taken from the case of Spain, where nominations to the Tribunal Constitucional have to be supported both by the majority and the opposition, as described in chapter 6. Applying this principle could ensure a balanced composition which would give equal attention to the concerns of both traditions.

44.   Human rights require that everyone within the nation shall have the same rights to political representation. In societies deeply divided by ethnic, religious or linguistic affiliations, this is not a simple matter. Two requirements should be fulfilled: (a) that the political system should ensure peaceful group accommodation; (b) that each of the groups can be ensured respect for their identity and their justified interests.

45.   Pure majoritarian governance in divided societies constitutes a serious threat to group accommodation. This is now widely recognized. Two options, or a combination, can help: (a) consociational democracy, including electoral systems which create ongoing incentives for inter-ethnic cooperation, and (b) in some cases territorial sub-division through federal systems or autonomies.

46.   Consociational democracy is built on the principle of executive power-sharing and a certain degree of self-administration for each group, whether they live together or separately. But it does cause problems, one of which is that it tends to freeze ethnic identities and lead to long-term polarization.

47.   The idea of power-sharing can be made much more flexible, to refer in more general terms to the quest for balanced representation in national institutions. Appropriate electoral systems are crucial in this regard, and there are numerous alternatives available when current practice in different countries is examined. Preference should be given to electoral systems which provide incentives for accommodative practices rather than to mobilize political support for ethnic extremism, and the system should encourage such accommodation in the run-up to elections, rather than through bargaining between the groups after the representatives have been elected on purely ethnic or communal grounds.

48.   Most of continental Europe has opted for proportional representation formulas, in contrast to single-member districts with plurality voting, while systems modelled on Anglo-American practice employ variations of the first-past-the-post plurality formulas. The Westminster model plurality system has lost standing. There are many cultural circumstances where its impact is perverse; Northern Ireland (where it still operates for Westminster elections, though not otherwise) is an obvious case. If communal voting patterns are preponderant, and the party system is rooted in cultural segments, its tendency to overrepresent majorities and to underrepresent minorities is a major shortcoming.

49.   Even if a majority were in some future to wish for and consent to the establishment of a united Ireland, the society in Northern Ireland would still be divided. Special arrangements would have to be made to ensure equality across the groups, including effective political participation through special electoral measures and arrangements within the judiciary and the security forces to ensure equality in the administration of justice and order.

50.   This includes, inter alia, arrangements ensuring a balanced composition of security forces, of the courts, and of all other agencies relating to the administration of justice. It also applies to political arrangements concerning the executive and the legislature, including the necessity for proportional rather than majority voting and the necessity for weighted voting, a point which is discussed at greater length in chapter 4.

EQUALITY AND NON-DISCRIMINATION

51.   Chapter 4 examines the elements of the comprehensive package, which with appropriate modifications, ought to be implemented in order to facilitate group accommodations in divided societies. The elements are threefold: equality in the common domain, pluralism in togetherness and, under some circumstances, territorial subdivisions based on democratic principles.

52.   A basic condition for peaceful accommodation is not only equality among individuals but also equal respect for the traditions and identities of each group, within the framework of universally recognized human rights. In multicultural or divided societies there is a need for two layers or levels of identity: at one level, a common identity for everyone living within the territory, to ensure the existence of a common

domain in which everybody can enjoy equally their individual human rights; on another level, acceptance of the existence of separate, ethnically or culturally based national identities, each of which is equally respected by the other side.

53.   Peaceful and constructive solutions to group accommodation and minority situations must start with effective measures to ensure equality and non-discrimination in the common domain within the national society. Members of the United Nations are generally obliged under the Charter to participate in the protection and promotion of human rights. By ratifying international human rights conventions, State parties undertake to respect and ensure the human rights contained in the convention concerned.

54.   Under the International Convention on Elimination of All Forms of Racial Discrimination (ICERD), States undertake to eliminate racial discrimination and promote understanding among all races. Racial discrimination includes ethnic or national discrimination. Whenever the word race is used in reference to ICERD, it includes national or ethnic origin. It can generally be assumed, with regard to national legislation, that the prohibition on the grounds of race also prohibits discrimination on grounds of national or ethnic origin. Since the purpose of ICERD is to prevent racial discrimination and this term includes ethnic origin, ICERD can be seen as the primary instrument for the promotion of equality between members of the different ethnic groups.

55.   The obligation to ensure equality implies that every State must guarantee the existence of a common domain open to all equally, not directed and controlled by the demands, symbols or practices of any one ethnic group or one religion to the exclusion of others. In the common domain, every resident must be equally free to participate and to enjoy their human rights without being treated as a second class resident or citizen due to her or his ethnic, religious, linguistic or national background.

56.   States have therefore undertaken to prohibit practices of racial and ethnic segregation; to prohibit and punish acts of violence or incitement to such acts against any race or group of another colour or ethnic origin; to prohibit organizations which incite to racial and thereby also to ethnic discrimination, and participation in such organizations.

57.   States have undertaken to guarantee the equal enjoyment by everyone of their rights in most aspects of their social, economic, political and cultural existence; equal treatment

before tribunals and other organs administering justice; equal rights to security of person and protection by the State against violence or bodily harm, whether inflicted by government officials or by any individual group or institutions; equal political rights; equal civil rights; equal enjoyment of economic, social and cultural rights, which include the right to equal participation in cultural activities and the right of equal access to any place or service intended for use by the general public.

58.   For this to be possible, however, a functioning democracy is required. The State must also respect the existence and promote conditions for the existence of a vigorous civil society. Networks across ethnic groups, formed by associations and non-governmental organizations of various kinds, are essential to withstand the destructive consequences of ethnic, linguistic or religious cleavages.

59.   For everybody living within Northern Ireland, as indeed in the whole of the United Kingdom or Ireland, human rights would have to be enjoyed on an equal basis. This follows, under international law, from the obligations undertaken by the United Kingdom and the Republic of Ireland as parties to the Covenants on Civil and Political Rights, and on Economic, Social and Cultural Rights. Under Article 2 of the Covenant on Civil and Political Rights, the rights shall be ensured to '… all individuals within its territory and subject to its jurisdiction …' and there shall be no distinction of any kind, such as '… language, religion, political or other opinion, national or social origin …'. The same principle of non-discrimination is also set out in defining State obligations under Article 2 of the International Covenant on Economic, Social and Cultural Rights.

60.   Special attention must be given to the prevention of discrimination in the administration of justice, including the role and performance of security forces, police and agents of prosecution, as well as the judiciary. Past experience has shown that few phenomena are more likely to create ethnic or national tension and violence than partiality in law enforcement. If members of one group feel that they do not get equal protection by the law, it can lead to self-defence measures which quickly generate conflict.

SPECIAL MEASURES AND COLLECTIVE RIGHTS

61.   A large part of relevant human rights law, including that dealing with minority rights, is 'soft' law. It conveys only some minimum obligations which have to be

respected, but in addition contains a number of *desiderata* — moral encouragement to take further steps. The United Nations Minority Declaration of 1992 and the Framework Convention for the Protection of Minorities of the Council of Europe (1994) can offer guidance. The language contained in the provisions leaves the State a wide discretion. This should be put to good use. There is no reason why that discretion shall be interpreted in its minimalist sense. Thus, even where explicit obligations cannot be deduced from the text, measures can and should be adopted to the extent that they do not conflict with other aspects of human rights, in particular the rights of others.

62.   The description of desirable lines of action in chapter 4 reflects not only the minimal requirements, but those measures which also best conform with the spirit of the international instruments in the field.

63.   This study notes that while international law generally does not recognize non-State collective rights which can be pursued at the international level, there is no general obstacle in international law to the existence of collective rights at the national level. International law provides only certain limitations that have to be observed in the establishment of such collective rights: firstly, they must not be of such a nature as to constitute racial or ethnic discrimination as defined under the Convention on the Elimination of Racial Discrimination, Article 1, nor must the group rights be of such a nature as to block the enjoyment of individuals belonging to that group of their individual human rights. There is, however, large scope for accommodation between these concerns. All human rights instruments related to minorities and groups emphasize that the right to belong or not to belong to a minority is a question of individual choice, and no adverse consequences shall arise from such choice.

64.   The search for multicultural pluralism combines efforts to ensure equal opportunity for everyone in the common society with programmes to allocate resources, power and space for separate groups. It requires tolerance and encouragement of ethnic political parties as part of the political system, in order that the different communal groups can participate in power-sharing or at least have an impact on decision-making, yet it also requires the existence of brokerage, of cross-ethnic or cross-religious alliances concerned with issues other than ethnicity or religion.

65.   The Declaration on the Rights of National or Ethnic, Religious and Linguistic Minorities, adopted by consensus by the General Assembly on 18 December 1992, is at present the main guide to evaluating State practice. The protection of minorities requires special measures which might appear to introduce discrimination between individuals belonging to majorities versus minorities. This issue must be handled with caution.

66.   The widely known case of *Brown v Board of Education* (1954) 347 US 483, referred to a situation where 'separate but equal' was an obvious cover-up for unequal treatment. It was also an unwanted separation. Collective rights must be such that they are not exclusive; options must exist for both those who want to join integrated schools and those who prefer separated schools, of their own volition and not due to lack of resources. Resources must be made equally available to each.

67.   The 1992 United Nations Declaration on the Rights of Persons Belonging to National or Ethnic, Religious and Linguistic Minorities states in Article 8 para. 2 that 'The exercise of the rights set forth in this Declaration shall not prejudice the enjoyment by all persons of universally recognized human rights and fundamental freedoms.'

68.   Not all distinctions, however, constitute discrimination. To explore this more fully, the concept of discrimination is analysed in chapter 4, and it is shown that special measures and communal rights can be formulated in ways which avoid discrimination against others.

69.   In so far as United Nations law is concerned, this has been clarified by the 1992 Minority Declaration, which states in Article 8 para. 3:

> Measures taken by States to ensure the effective enjoyment of the rights set forth in this Declaration shall not *prima facie* be considered contrary to the principle of equality contained in the Universal Declaration of Human Rights.

70.   Controversies surrounding the question of collective rights is due in part to a lack of distinction between different issues involved. At least three aspects are examined in chapter 4: (a) are the beneficiaries defined as individuals or groups? (b) under domestic or under international law? (c) if groups are beneficiaries, do they

also have a formal standing under applicable procedural law, and who are entitled to represent them?

71. In so far as minorities are concerned, the consistent practice in standard-setting activities, at the level of the United Nations, in the Council of Europe, and in the Organization for Security and Co-operation in Europe, is to use the formulation 'persons belonging'. The direct beneficiaries, therefore, are defined as individuals, not groups.

72. There is no requirement or obligation under international law which prevents States from introducing collective rights in their internal legislation in order to promote group accommodation and minority protection. Some of the rights recognized under international law, while expressed as rights of individuals, can best be implemented if groups are entitled to deal with those rights under national law. Consequently, States may recognize particular groups, allow them to establish their own agencies, and under domestic law deal with those agencies who then act on behalf of the individuals. This is done in the jurisdiction of many countries and there is nothing strange about it.

PRESERVATION OF IDENTITY: LANGUAGE, CULTURE AND EDUCATION

73. States are called upon under Article 1 of the Minority Declaration to take the necessary legislative measures to protect their existence and identity and to encourage conditions for the promotion of that identity. In doing so, States may consider it necessary to mention the specific groups which are the intended beneficiaries of the legislation. There is a risk that such legislation could exclude some groups. This can be avoided by referring to abstract criteria for the existence of minorities, rather than by naming them.

74. The protection and promotion of the cultural and spiritual dimensions of existence are also fundamental to the Declaration. In the past, minority groups were sometimes effectively denied their 'existence' through policies of forced assimilation or ethnocide. It is now generally recognized, in line with the evolution within UNESCO on these matters, that each culture has a dignity and value which must be respected and preserved, to the extent compatible with universal human rights.

RIGHT TO USE OWN LANGUAGE IN CONTACTS WITH AUTHORITIES AND COURTS

75.   It is important for members of minorities to be able to address courts of law and other authorities in their own language, in order to feel secure that their own language is sufficient to be able to function in society and thus to be at ease in preserving their own identity. In practice, it is generally accepted that minorities can use their own language in regard to courts and authorities within territorial units of the State in which that minority language is prominent or is very widely used.

PRESERVATION AND DEVELOPMENT OF MINORITY CULTURE

76.   Culture includes the cultural environment, including street names and toponyms. Under the Framework Convention for the Protection of National Minorities of the Council of Europe, Article 11(3), States shall endeavour '… to display traditional local names, street names and other topographical indications intended for the public also in the minority language where there is a sufficient demand for such indications.'

77.   In chapter 4, national practice in several countries providing for such displays of names and other indications by the communal groups is reviewed.

EDUCATION IN MULTICULTURAL SOCIETIES

78.   States should take measures in the field of education to encourage knowledge of the history, traditions, language and culture of the national minorities existing within that territory. Persons belonging to such minorities should have adequate opportunities to gain knowledge of their society as a whole.

79.   The Convention on the Rights of the Child, Article 29, which spells out the threefold requirement for education can offer guidance. States parties to the Convention agree that the education of the child shall be directed to:

>   (c) The development of respect for the child's parents, his or her own cultural identity, for the national values of the country in which the child is living, the country from which he or she may originate and for civilizations different from his or her own.

The next paragraph is also important:

> (d) The preparation of the child for responsible life in a free society, in the spirit of understanding, peace, tolerance, equality of sexes, and friendship among all peoples, ethnic, national and religious groups and persons of indigenous origins.

CONTACTS ACROSS BORDERS

80. Transfrontier contacts now form part of generally recognized human rights. The right to contact with members of kin groups in other countries is specifically mentioned both in the OSCE documents and in the United Nations Minority Declaration. Such contacts are not a privilege but an uncontroversial right. States should not, and most States do not, prevent persons belonging to a national minority from having free and unimpeded contacts with those citizens of another country with whom the minority shares ethnic, religious or linguistic features or a cultural identity.

81. Within the territory of the divided Ireland there are particularly strong reasons, now that violence has come to a halt, to establish comprehensive economic, cultural and other forms of interaction and cooperation including communications. While some such contacts are of an unofficial nature, there is nothing in international law preventing the establishment of elaborate State-to-State structures as provided for in the Anglo-Irish Agreement or as envisaged in the Joint Declaration and *A New Framework for Agreement*.

ROLES FOR THE INTERNATIONAL COMMUNITY

82. Bilateral treaties containing clauses on protection of minorities can be useful for peaceful group accommodation if they provide a more satisfactory protection of minorities and serve to reduce or prevent tension between the kin State and the home State of the minorities concerned.

83. The Paris Conference on Stability, convened by the European Union on the initiative of the former French Prime Minister, Mr Balladur on 20-21 March 1995, focused on the need for bilateral and multilateral processes of consultations and negotiations by which States could resolve their problems concerning borders and group accommodation. The planned projects concern regional transborder cooperation,

questions relating to minorities, cultural cooperation, including language training, regional economic cooperation, legal cooperation and administrative training, as well as environmental problems.

84. The pact relies heavily on the use of bilateral treaties regulating good neighbourly relations including provisions for minority protection and group accommodation. The present study reviews the discussions on the usefulness of such treaties. They are not always helpful, but in some circumstances they can be very constructive. For them to be so, the treaties should provide for the establishment of mechanisms at the governmental level to supervise of the application of the treaty. Various possibilities can be taken into consideration, including political consultations and joint commissions.

85. Regarding Northern Ireland and its wider Irish and British contexts, the provisions in the Anglo-Irish Agreement of 1985, the Joint Declaration and the proposals set out in *A New Framework for Agreement* (were they or equivalent arrangements to be adopted) constitute probably one of the most interesting examples presently existing of how bilateral approaches could actually or potentially assist in resolving group conflict and consolidating stability in Europe. The threefold approach, emphasizing that structures in Northern Ireland must depend on the cooperation of elected representatives there on the basis of cross-community agreement; that North-South institutions should be established on the island of Ireland as a whole, which enable the representatives of the main traditions in the North and South to cooperate; and finally the East-West cooperative structures between the two islands, through a standing intergovernmental conference, appear to provide a very advanced example of the way in which bilateral arrangements could develop in other circumstances.

THE EUROPEAN UNION AND GROUP ACCOMMODATION WITHIN MEMBER STATES

86. It has frequently been noted that the Maastricht option, through the application of the subsidiarity principle whereby some powers are transferred to the central authorities while others are devolved to sub-national authorities, might encourage decentralization and legitimize transboundary regional cooperation. This could facilitate close economic, cultural and other links by minorities and nationalities in the home State with populations in the kin State.

87. An additional factor is free movement of labour, investment and trade, all of which facilitates desired linkages far beyond anything that has existed in the more rigid

periods of State formation. These options, however, are so far mainly available in the European community, but they already existed in such regional arrangements as the Nordic Council and in Benelux. Most ethnically based minorities in Western Europe support the European Union because of these facilities for greater decentralization and transboundary cooperation.

88. Under the Treaty on European Union, Article 128 (1) has established a Community responsibility not only for respecting the national and regional diversity within the Union, but also for contributing to the flowering of the cultures of the member States.

THE COUNCIL OF EUROPE AND OSCE

89. International institutions may be helpful in assisting the development of legal mechanisms required for group accommodation inside States. The rich experience of different countries, collected and systematized within the Council of Europe and to a lesser extent within the United Nations Centre for Human Rights, could be drawn upon in the form of advisory services and through the organization of training seminars for relevant parts of the civil service and the media.

90. The Council of Europe is likely to be of greater significance in the future, when full human rights compliance can be required in more normal circumstances. Armed confrontations have now ended, and past justification for the use of emergency legislation no longer applies. Consequently, derogations from human rights obligations under international law can no longer be made. It is of particular importance for the Governments to ensure that their law enforcement officials comply with the requirements contained in international human rights instruments, including the Code of Conduct for Law Enforcement Officials and the Principles on the Use of Force and Firearms by Law Enforcement Officials, as described below in chapter 4.

91. With regard to international monitoring of compliance with minority or communal rights, the future additional protocol on cultural rights to the European convention may bring some of the main controversial issues under international control.

92. Similarly, in the process of peaceful accommodation within Northern Ireland, the offices of the High Commissioner on Minorities of the OSCE, Mr Max van der

Stoel, might in the future be drawn upon by the parties. His mandate excluded him in the past from involvement as long as acts of violence continued, but since organized violence has ceased, his mandate would cover Northern Ireland, if so desired by the Governments concerned. He could not, on the other hand, deal with issues relating to self-determination and change of borders, which would fall outside his mandate.

93.   It should be noted, in general, that international agencies are at present not equipped to deal with disputes over the right to self-determination involving claims for secession or change of borders. As shown above, however, they might sometimes be useful either in facilitating peaceful accommodation between groups within established borders or in assisting the parties to find appropriate solutions after a decision has been made, by consent, to redraw the borders by changing the territorial arrangements between sovereign States.

1. Territorial Disputes and Policies in Plural Societies

Group conflicts can involve two basic issues: territorial control and policies of integration versus separation. In this chapter, the focus will be on categories of policies pursued by States towards the different elements of plural societies. Issues connected with territorial disputes will be dealt with in chapter 3, where the focus is on the contradictions between territorial integrity of States and self-determination of peoples.

Within national societies, there is normally a drive towards integration, which can be effected in different ways. In some situations, however, separation or even exclusion are emphasized. These categories are explored below.

1.1 Homogenization

This process (making everybody alike, i.e. seeking to make everyone conform to one common culture, one language, one set of mores and behaviour) can be pursued in two ways: through fusion and through assimilation.

Fusion is, in theory, different from assimilation. It consists of a process whereby a combination of two or more cultures, on an equal basis, produces a new and different culture. It corresponds to the more popular notion of the 'melting pot' and occurs mainly in immigrant settler societies, where the immigrants come from different nationalities and ethnic groups to make a new life. The indigenous peoples who lived there before, however, are rarely participants on an equal level in the process of fusion.

Assimilation is understood as homogenization with a dominant culture, to which other groups are expected to conform by shedding their own cultural characteristics. Although this is a dominating technique, it at least has the redeeming feature that it accepts new members. A fully inclusive, assimilationist approach would be anti-racist and non-discriminatory in all fields other than culture.

Exclusion is homogenization by an entirely different and much more reprehensible process, making the society homogenous by excluding those who belong to a different ethnic or religious group. The general term today for such policies is ethnic cleansing, which is pursued in more or less brutal ways. One approach is to deny citizenship, at the time of independence or restored independence, to long-standing resident members of another ethnic group or to make it difficult for them to obtain citizenship, combined with rules which prevent the denationalized residents from holding property and access to jobs in the public service;[1] a more brutal approach is to terrorize members of other ethnic groups in order to make them flee the territory;[2] a third approach is large-scale population transfers.[3] The extreme approach is genocide.[4]

1.2 INTEGRATION

This differs from homogenization. While separate elements do combine into a political and economic unity, each group retains its identity to the extent that it does not threaten the overarching unity. Two versions of integration should be examined: egalitarian integration and integration based on discrimination.

1.2.1 EGALITARIAN INTEGRATION:

Key indicators in practice of the difference between fusion or assimilation on the one hand, and egalitarian integration on the other, can be found in policies related to language and education. Policies of homogenization allow only one language for public use and for publicly funded education, and standardize the content of education within a common cultural frame to facilitate social interaction. Policies of egalitarian integration allow two or several languages or provide for publicly supported education in different languages where several linguistic groups coexist, allowing for public use also of non-official languages. Homogenizing educational policies seek to draw all members of society, through their education, into the common culture by transmitting a common set of values, a common conception of history and a common preferred future vision. By contrast integrationist policies give space for presentation of the different cultures and traditions in that society and the different conceptions of history, thus also allowing some scope for differences in future visions.

Integration can be based on one dominant culture. It is an intermediate policy between assimilation and separation. It can also be based on a process of fusion, where the fusion is not complete but allows for the preservation of separate group identity in some respects.

Ideally, the purpose of integration is to guarantee the same rights and opportunity to all citizens, whatever their group membership, while allowing them to maintain differences which do not threaten the existence of an all-embracing national society. Integration is possible only when ethnic or cultural cleavages are secondary to common social values and loyalties.

1.2.2 INTEGRATION BY DISCRIMINATION AND UNEQUAL TREATMENT

Majority policies sometimes reflect patterns of discrimination: unequal treatment, denial of access to certain jobs, to housing in certain areas, or other forms. It can include separation, in schools, in means of transport, and in other ways. Discrimination is not necessarily imposed by law. In many places it results from widespread practice by members of the majority, when the State fails to protect against discrimination.

There are examples of a two-pronged approach where the main policy is one of fusion or assimilation on a basis of equality, but where members of some groups are integrated on a basis of inequality, being offered only the lower jobs and inferior education and being subjected to other negative measures. The purpose then is not to exclude those members from participating in the economic life of society, but to make use of them in an exploitative pattern, mainly on racial lines.

1.3 PLURALIST ACCOMMODATION

Policies of partial integration might be combined with some degree of separate functional autonomy, recognizing the separate existence of different groups on a non-territorial basis. Members of groups dispersed in society may want to be given separate treatment in some aspects of their life, while living with others on common territory. This is practised extensively in different parts of the world. After centuries of conflict, solutions have been found recently in most cases with regard to religion. The existence and separate management of religious places of worship (churches, mosques, synagogues and temples) and religious organizations are broadly accepted today, though they still give rise to considerable tension in some places.

Controversies regarding the use of language and content of education are more difficult. A variety of approaches can be found in multicultural societies, including separate schools, or separate classes for some parts of the curriculum. The concern with equality, in particular equal opportunities in the larger society, poses problems in the implementation even of well-intentioned pluralist policies. To find the appropriate balance between partial separateness and equality is a task of considerable complexity.

Pluralist group accommodation may also be based on a ranking system: dispossessed groups deprived of large parts of their land or other resources are, in a pattern of benign neglect, left to their own devices by a system of self-government but without access to the resources necessary to give substance to their self-government. There is a risk that some arrangements for dispossessed indigenous groups might fall into this category.

1.4 SEPARATION

1.4.1 SUBDIVISION

Territorial subdivisions, which respect the territorial integrity of the State as a whole, constitute another line of action. Territorial separation can be a solution on an egalitarian basis, where dissimilar groups voluntarily choose to live territorially apart within the same sovereign State, and the territorial separation is made in order to better preserve their own particular lifestyles and cultures, while in some respects they form partners in a larger entity on a basis of equality and non-discrimination.

This is effected on an egalitarian basis provided (a) that it is indeed the voluntary choice of each group involved; (b) that there is no hierarchical ranking between the groups; (c) that they share common resources on a basis of equality; and (d) wherever they interact, there are no privileges for members of one group and exclusions or restrictions for members of other groups.

Territorial subdivision can also be pursued on a basis of ranking, or discrimination. The extreme version of dominant separation is that of *segregation*, the prime example being *apartheid*, which aims at keeping the ethnic groups territorially separate, unmixed, and ranked in a hierarchical position. This policy was used for purposes of extreme exploitation, by depriving the weaker groups of access to resources except on conditions set by the dominant group. Segregation is a flagrant violation of human rights.

The establishment of autonomies is one approach which might be egalitarian but in many cases is not because it could be preferential for the dominant group within the autonomous area, facilitating discrimination or even exclusion of members of ethnic groups. Consequently, there is a need to analyse the policies of majorities within autonomies in the same way as we analyse the policies of majorities within the State as a whole.

1.4.2 TERRITORIAL DISMEMBERMENT

Breaking a sovereign State into two or more independent units, or transferring part of the territory to another State, is one possible approach to group accommodation; it is, however, in most cases associated with severe violence and causes great suffering for many members of society.

On rare occasions, territorial dismemberment may be the result of a peaceful process of reciprocal withdrawal from the common State. The dissolution of Czechoslovakia in 1992 is the most recent example. Even when it is peaceful and negotiated, it can cause serious problems or fears for some members of society. The dissolution of Czechoslovakia has caused difficulties for the gypsies living in the Czech Republic, and has made the Hungarians in Slovakia apprehensive. If properly done, however, dismemberment as a result of peaceful negotiations may make it possibile to sort out human rights aspects prior to the dissolution. Cases of unilateral secession are much more problematic. Dominant groups within the area which secedes often engage in ethnic cleansing as part of secessionist violence, forcing members of other ethnic groups to flee the contested territory altogether.

2. GROUP CONFLICTS AND CLAIMS

A review of the various situations of divided societies and group conflicts, shows that they take many different forms and that they change over time. This chapter seeks to explore the main categories of conflict. Different situations require different responses. Using the same approach to vastly different situations aggravates rather than ameliorates the tension between groups. If lessons are to be drawn from approaches which have been successful or disastrous in other situations, it is necessary to bear in mind that each conflict has its own character and can never be fully equated with others. That said, it can be helpful to try to categorize conflicts and to look at the appropriate responses to each.

2.1 CATEGORIES OF CONFLICTS AND SITUATIONS

ETHNO-CLASSES

One category arises as a result of systematic discrimination against persons because of their colour, race, ethnicity or religion. The reference here is to groups whose members struggle to obtain equal enjoyment, as individuals, of civil, political, economic and social rights. Discrimination arises when the majority, or the dominant part of society, seeks to impede their equal enjoyment of these rights.

IDENTITY

A second category arises when members of a particular group, while seeking equality in the enjoyment of human rights also seek to preserve their own ethnic, cultural or linguistic identity and to develop it. Conflicts arise when the dominant group, while accepting the other group's right to equal treatment as individuals, seek to block it from opportunities to preserve and develop its identity in a way comparable to that which the dominant group enjoys.

RELIGION

A third category occurs when a group is identified by the particular religion to which its members adhere, which differs from that of the dominant group, and when there is tension between the two religions. It is not simply a question of religious intolerance by the dominant group. There may also be a fear within the majority that should the other religion come to dominate, its adherents might themselves become intolerant and repressive of other opinions and try to organize society in line with the particular premises of their religion.

ETHNIC OR COMMUNAL CONTENDERS

This is a concept introduced in a recent study by Ted Gurr.[1] The contenders are 'culturally distinct peoples, tribes, or clans, in heterogeneous societies who hold or seek a share in State power'. Ethnic contenders do not necessarily seek cultural or linguistic dominance over the national society, nor do they necessarily try to secede from the national society, but they seek to enhance their own position or maintain it when challenged by other contenders. This description fits the situation in some post-colonial societies, particularly in Africa, where borders were drawn rather arbitrarily by colonial powers in such a way that different tribes, culturally distinct clans or linguistic groups came to be included within the same State.

CENTRE-PERIPHERY CONFLICTS

A type of conflict which occurs frequently is that between a dominant centre and a peripheral group which is culturally distinct from that of the centre. A typical example, but not the only one, is the situation of indigenous peoples, groups whose traditional way of life is challenged by a dominant centre which exploits the resource base of local, vulnerable groups and in the process also destroys or weakens the capacity of that group to reproduce and to develop its own culture, including its language and religion. In recent decades such groups have mobilized in resistance and sought international support for their right to have a separate identity, a degree of self-government and control over their own resource base, in order to perpetuate and sustain their own culture and direction of development.

ETHNO-NATIONALISTS

The sixth type of conflict, and often the most difficult one, arises when two groups, defining themselves as nations in an ethnic sense, conflict with each other over the same territory. This includes situations where the majority does not define itself ethnically, but a substantial minority group does, and demands control over the territory in the name of that nation. Such conflicts become particularly severe because they involve not only questions of reciprocal adaptation to each other, but issues of exclusive or hegemonical control. These are the conflicts which receive most attention at present, ranging from Serbian efforts to obtain territorial control in parts of Bosnia and Croatia, to the efforts by the Armenian majority in Nagorno-Karabakh to secede from Azerbaijan, the Chechnian efforts to become independent of the Russian Federation, and the Tamil Tigers' efforts to gain exclusive control over a homeland in the north and east of Sri Lanka.

2.2 CLAIMS

Having defined the different types of conflict, we shall now examine the claims made in each of them, and in the subsequent sections explore the validity of such claims from the perspective of contemporary international law.

- Members of *ethno-classes* demand to be treated as equals in society, that there should be no distinction or exclusion based on their national or ethnic origin. They want equal enjoyment of civil and political rights; equal protection by the law and before any tribunal and all other organs administering justice; rights to personal security and protection by the State against violence or bodily harm; political rights including the right to participate in elections, to take part in the government and in the conduct of public affairs; economic and social rights in accordance with what they are entitled to under the international human rights system, on the basis of equality with all other members in society. If they have in the past been subjected to systematic discrimination, they may want transitional special measures to ensure adequate advancement of their potential to enjoy human rights on an equal level. This is often referred to as 'affirmative action', a subject to which we shall return.

- Turning to conflicts of *identity*, these centre on issues commonly referred to as minority claims. They include the right to exist and to preserve the identity of the group as such; the right to use one's mother tongue, in private and in public, and under some conditions a right to use it in their relationship with public authorities of the society concerned, which requires that the latter have the capacity to understand or to ensure interpretation to make it possible to communicate in that language. The claim may also include the right to learn one's own language, and even the right to be taught in one's own language at school, during different stages of education. Another set of claims concerns the right to manifest one's own culture, its symbols and its traditions.

- In conflicts over *religion* the minimum demand by a given religious group is to be free to have a religion or belief of their own choice, and freedom individually, or in community with others, and in public as well as private, to manifest the religion or belief in worship, observance and practice. Furthermore, members of such religions demand the right to organize life within the family in accordance with their religion or belief, and thereby also to determine the moral education of the child. Tension may arise, however, when the child joins the educational system. While the parents of the child may be entitled to object to the child being taught about values and beliefs different from their own, society at large may consider it important that the child becomes aware of other values and beliefs in society, and that everyone in society shares some common values without which the society could not function. Conflicts can become particularly serious if one or several religions aspire to obtain a hegemonical control also in secular matters.

- The competition for power between different *ethnic or communal contenders* is primarily due to lack of a democratic tradition and the ability to make the necessary compromises. A classic case is the developments in Nigeria in the 1960s, which led to the failed effort of secession by Biafra. The origin of that secession was not an intention to secede, but an attempt by the modernized Ibo army officers to take power in the whole of Nigeria through a military coup in January 1966. Their initial intention was to establish a unitary system of government for the whole of Nigeria. This resulted in a counter-coup in July 1966. Following the counter-coup, several senior Ibo officers were killed and serious atrocities took place in September and October 1966. This was the time at which the Ibo population in Biafra decided to try to secede from Nigeria, an effort which lasted for about a thousand days, from May 1967 until January 1970. The secessionists were defeated, but the net outcome was an extensive decentralization of Nigeria, providing considerable scope for ambitious political leaders in the different regions to obtain a political platform in their own provinces, thereby reducing the intensity of ethnic conflict in Nigeria as a whole.

In the territorially small countries of Rwanda and Burundi, the conflicts between the ethnic contenders of the Hutus and the Tutsis could not be solved in the same way, since they were territorially interspersed. The Hutu majority had been dominated by the less numerous Tutsis but when majoritarian government was introduced the Tutsis were unwilling to relinquish their privileges with the result that the Hutus' grievances led to frightening bloodshed.

- In the *centre-periphery conflicts*, typified by those of indigenous peoples, the minimum claims include freedom from discrimination; equality in the common domain; the right to maintain their own religious traditions and practices; to preserve their own culture and for that purpose to maintain control over the land and natural resources required to continue their way of life in accordance with their culture and to pursue a development policy in line with their own value systems, in particular their own attitude to the environment and the ecological balance. At most, this adds up to a demand for autonomy over the areas in which they live, combined with compensation for areas which have been taken away from them. In the ultimate case, there is a demand for full self-determination.

- The claims of *ethno-nationalists* are the most difficult, since they constitute conflict over territory. Experience shows that there are almost no ethnically homogeneous States. Whichever ethnic group controls a given territory, there is likely to be one or more minorities who might consider themselves discriminated against or treated as second-class citizens. Beyond demanding the traditional rights to preserve and develop their own identity, and to have parity of esteem with regard to identity, the preferred option of ethno-nationalists is to achieve a congruence between the State and the nation defined in ethnic terms. This may be expressed in claims of self-determination, translated either into demands for independence for the particular territory in which they live, a merger with a neighbouring State, or autonomy for the area in which they live. To explore guidelines for handling such situations, we turn in the next chapter to the principles of territorial integrity versus self-determination.

2.3 COMBINATIONS AND CHANGES OF CLAIMS

Different members of a given group may have different preferences and strategies. Some are satisfied with the achievement of equality of treatment and the right to preserve their own identity, while others may have maximalist claims, extending all the way to a demand for secession or unification with another country. A number of factors influence these attitudes, including the question of material incentives versus the values of ethnic identity. This plays itself out, in particular, with questions such as language education. When the language of a particular group is distinctly a minor language many of its members may be tempted to become fluent in the dominant language, in order to have better opportunities on the market for employment and other roles in society. Not surprisingly, therefore, a wide variety of claims can be seen within a given group. It depends also, to a large extent, on the responses by the dominant group. If the latter rejects even reasonable, minimal claims such as equality in treatment and the preservation of identity, particularly when resorting to repressive measures involving violence, the members of the minority group become much more internally consolidated, and the conflict more polarized.

When, by contrast, the rights of equal treatment and preservation of identity are accepted, this will in most situations lead to a decline in the intensity of the conflict. This, however, is not always the case, if the attraction for independence or joining another State is great, because of the material benefits of a higher standard of living and greater opportunities in the other territory, equal enjoyment of human rights and conditions allowing the preservation of identity will not suffice. This is one reason for a certain fear of granting advanced cultural rights and autonomy to Hungarians living in Romania and Slovakia, who might be attracted by Hungarian society. Past experiences of extreme persecution may also be a factor in continuing the quest for independence even when substantial rights are given, as in the case of the Armenians in Nagorno-Karabakh who have suffered tragedies in previous generations.

3. SOVEREIGNTY, TERRITORIAL INTEGRITY AND SELF-DETERMINATION

The following discussion is based on contemporary principles of international law, mainly as found in the United Nations Charter.

3.1 THE CONTENT AND PARADOXES OF SOVEREIGNTY WITHIN THE EMERGING WORLD ORDER [1]

The Charter of the United Nations is based on the system of sovereign States. In one sense it aims to strengthen national sovereignty; in another sense, it makes sovereignty qualitatively different, more open and less absolute than formerly. This apparent paradox needs to be examined since it helps to explain the importance of the guidelines on which this study is based.

Strengthening of national sovereignty has resulted primarily from efforts by the United Nations to protect all sovereign States against aggression or the use of force against their territorial integrity and political independence. This is further developed in a number of related normative instruments, including the elaboration of the principle of non-intervention. Generally speaking, the development of large parts of international law serves to strengthen national sovereignty by ensuring that more powerful States deal with weaker States according to mutually agreed law rather than by force.

The extension of the sovereignty of States, however, is linked to the acceptance of evolving international law. Just as freedom for individuals cannot exist without some form of organized order administered by the State, the enjoyment of sovereignty by States cannot exist without some degree of international order. The Charter and the instruments adopted on the basis of the Charter have also changed the content and quality of sovereignty. This can best be understood by taking into account that States, as distinct from individuals, are composite entities.

The legitimate function of States is to advance the welfare and freedom of their inhabitants. States therefore have responsibilities under international law not only in regard to other States, but also to the individuals under their jurisdiction. They are obliged to respect, protect and fulfil the human rights of their own inhabitants. While States may retain a formal freedom to adopt the constitutional and legislative provisions of their own choice, they are already subordinated to international requirements which to a significant degree limit that choice. They can seek to deviate from the international principles but only at their own cost as they increasingly find that this adversely affects the possibility of participating in international cooperation in other fields.

The source of sovereignty has also changed. In earlier periods, it was considered to derive from the lawful prince or whoever held effective power in the State. The contemporary system of international human rights law is based on the principle of popular sovereignty. The source of authority is the will of the people, which requires regular and free elections with universal suffrage. Sovereignty, then, is exercised by the representatives elected by the people.

They also have to respect the transnational links that individuals, groups and associations within the jurisdiction of their State have with individuals, groups and associations in other countries. In this way there develops a criss-crossing network and a set of interests which no single State can regulate entirely on its own. Consequently, joint regulation has become increasingly necessary; in order to have influence in those matters which affect issues normally thought to be within their own jurisdiction, States have to accept that other States also have influence and that compromises and common policies increasingly have to be found.

Equality in the enjoyment of sovereignty includes respect for the control by other States over resources within their jurisdiction. This also requires that these States, for their part, respect limits to activities which have transboundary environmental effects.

The demand for sovereignty, if taken seriously, therefore, makes it necessary to accept limits to sovereignty. It is a reflection of this need that there has in recent decades been a tremendous growth in international legislation, step by step limiting the scope of State sovereignty.

As this study explores these issues from a human rights perspective, two major and partly conflicting obligations of the State bring those issues into central focus: the State is obliged to ensure equality in the enjoyment of human rights for all its residents, but is also increasingly considered obliged to respect and protect the existence and identity of groups.

3.2 THE MULTICULTURAL REALITY AND WORLD ORDER

National societies almost everywhere are multicultural; there is, however, in many places an unwillingness to accept this fact. What is more, there is considerable confusion about the nature of our multicultural reality. These issues are discussed more fully in chapter 5; here, only some brief comments will be made.

Societies are multicultural not simply because groups with different cultural identities coexist within the same State. Our multicultural legacy is shared by every group. Everyone is affected by layers of culture which criss-cross. The main religions have contributed to the formation of broad civilizations; the civilizations have affected and influenced each other to a substantial degree. Within those civilizations and sometimes cutting across them are several linguistic cultures; there are combined or fused cultures such as the Afro-American which is the product of the experience of the black population in the American culture. It is scarcely possible for anyone to single out one culture with which they can identify in all respects.

The increasing trend towards multiculturalism arises from several factors. Migration, changes in communications technology, the ever expanding role of the media. Since at least the beginning of the modern period,[2] there has been a process of globalization, which is gathering pace. The trend to globalization is irreversible but it can also provoke conflict. It is irreversible because we cannot be fully insulated from one another. The concern for the environment, to mention just one factor, and with the carrying capacity of spaceship earth, makes it abundantly clear that we have a common destiny, and that we have to find ways of coping with globalization while maintaining the existence and identity of our particular communities.

Globalization is also aggressive, for several reasons. For example, it has often in the past tended to favour the strong at the expense of the weak and the process has yielded different results for different participants. The technologically and organizationally dominant societies have gained considerable benefits from globalization; others have been further impoverished or denied their equal share in its benefits.

The United Nations Secretary-General, Boutros Boutros-Ghali, noted in *An Agenda for Peace*, 1992, para. 1, that respect for the fundamental sovereignty and integrity of States is crucial to any common international progress. He noted also, however, that the time of absolute and exclusive sovereignty has passed; its theory was never matched by reality.

The borders of existing States are not sacrosanct. The promotion and consolidation of the rule of law, however, require their existence and stability unless and until such time as change can peacefully take place through the consent of those affected. For States to play a constructive role as intermediaries between the individual, groups and the international order, they have to conform to certain general principles, primarily derived from the Charter of the United Nations as elaborated by its competent bodies.

3.3   TERRITORIAL INTEGRITY

A major objective of the Charter of the United Nations was to outlaw the use of force and to prevent intervention directed against the territorial integrity and political independence of States,[3] which is also applicable in situations of group conflict inside a State. The emphasis on territorial integrity is contained not only in the United Nations Charter and the Declaration on Friendly Relations, but also in regional instruments. The CSCE Final Act Principle IV is an explicit endorsement of the principle. The Council of Europe has repeatedly stressed the paramount importance of this principle. In the Declaration emerging from the Summit Meeting of Heads of State and Governments of the Council of Europe, held in Vienna 1993, its members commit themselves to the protection of the rights of national minorities 'within the rule of law, respecting the territorial integrity and the national sovereignty of States.' The principle of non-intervention in situations of group conflict is essential to international peace, but it must be complemented by a sincere effort, by all States, to build confidence and promote equality among the different ethnic, religious and linguistic groups in the national society.

It will be shown below, under the discussion of the principle of self-determination, that changes in territory can be fully legitimate and conform with international law if they are achieved through consent between those affected. In some cases there are particularly strong justifications for such change.

3.3.1 AUTONOMY ARRANGEMENTS

Territorial integrity does not exclude the possibility of autonomy arrangements within sovereign States, or local control over natural and other resources when this is required to ensure the livelihood of endangered and vulnerable groups. In recent years the question of control over land and natural resources has formed a prominent part during the arrangements made for indigenous peoples. This was one of the issues precipitating the conflict between the Sandinista Government of Nicaragua and the Indian communities of the Atlantic coast from 1979 until in 1986 autonomy status was adopted.[4] Given that under many legal systems the State is deemed to possess primordial title to sub-surface resources, governments sometimes take the view that even putting the issue on the agenda for discussion undermines the very idea of an overarching national sovereignty. One of the most extreme legal systems in this respect was the Australian, which postulated that the area taken from the population living there when British settlers arrived was *terra nullius*, without ownership, and that consequently land belonged either to the settlers or to the Crown (the State). In recent years, however, greater flexibility has been shown, also in the legal systems of States, in recognizing the collective right to land, particularly of indigenous peoples. In Australia, the High Court decision of June 1992 (*Mabo v Queensland*) recognized aboriginal land rights and declared that they had never been extinguished.[5] Restoration or compensation may gradually follow.

3.3.2 THE 'PEOPLE' AS THE BASIS OF AUTHORITY

While States have obligations to respect, protect and fulfil human rights for all their inhabitants, those inhabitants are themselves the source of government power: 'The will of the people shall be the basis of the authority of the government.'[6] The right to the full participation in political life of all individuals and groups, as provided for in the two international covenants and in the Universal Declaration, is essential. There are two aspects to this. One is that government should be based on the participation of members of all ethnic or religious groups, not by only one of them. There has to be democracy, not ethnocracy, not even by the majority ethnic group. The second aspect is that the participation of the different groups must be effective; a formal participation is not enough if the minority groups are consistently outvoted by majority representatives. The act of balancing between majoritarian decisions and proper attention to the demands of minorities constitutes a core element in the majority/minority relationship.

3.4 EXTERNAL ACTORS AND INTERNATIONAL SOCIETY

3.4.1 INTERVENTION AND REGIONAL CONFLICTS

Ethnic or religious conflicts can easily lead to regional and international tension, and in some cases to overt intervention, with its profoundly destabilizing effects for international peace. Intervention may be initiated by the 'mother country' or kin State (see chapter 10) with the claim that its ethnic relatives are subjected to intolerable violations. Intervention can be open or disguised, including the organization, assistance, fomenting, financing, incitement or tolerance of subversive, terrorist or armed activities directed towards the violent overthrow of the regime of another State or interference in the civil strife of another State through such behaviour.[7]

In recent years, there has been a growing emphasis on the notion of 'common security', manifested by a climate of close and constructive cooperation among States. While global common security is far in the future, there are numerous regional areas of common security, sometimes called 'security communities' because of the cooperation and reciprocal trust arising from joint management of matters of common concern. One major area of common concern is the treatment of nationalities which live as a minority in one State and a majority in a neighbouring State. This can easily become a source of tension between the two States, but it can also become a constructive link for cooperation.

A regional and international climate of stability is essential in the process of expanding cooperation aimed at creating conditions where the common goal is to bring about freedom from want (economic and social rights) and freedom from fear (i.e. security policies which are much more cooperative and less confrontational than those of the past). Peaceful and constructive approaches to minority issues are therefore essential also for the realization of economic and social rights for all.

3.5 SELF-DETERMINATION

A claim to self-determination constitutes one among several possible approaches to group relations. Taking into account that societies are increasingly multicultural and that to an ever increasing degree members of different groups live interspersed with each other, the choice of platform and strategy have far-reaching consequences for human rights and social peace.

The right to self-determination cannot be meaningfully discussed in general and abstract terms. It is necessary to examine the different contexts in which claims to self-determination are made, in order to assess their validity in each circumstance and in the light of other relevant principles and of the options available.

Claims to self-determination have been made mainly in three categories of situation: (a) non-self-governing territories, including occupied territories; (b) independent countries where the population for some reason is unable to govern itself; (c) parts of a territory of a sovereign State where an ethnic group challenges the legitimacy of the central government to exercise authority over that group.

There is near-universal consensus that the population of non-self-governing and occupied territories has a right to self-determination; the main content of the right is to determine the political status of the territory as a whole. In these cases, the beneficiary of the right (the 'people') is the population of the territory as a whole. The integrity of the territory must be respected; the right to self-determination therefore does not give separate parts of the population of any part of the non-self-governing territory a right to break out of the territory, and if the territory is to be divided it must be on the basis of agreement between the constituent groups of the population.

There is a broadening consensus that the population in every independent country (the 'people' as a whole), has a right to self-determination. The content of the right is to be able to determine the economic, social and cultural development of the country concerned. This means that the population must have an effective democratic system of governance where all parts of the population participate. It must be underlined that the beneficiary of this right is the people as a whole, meaning that members of the different ethnic, religious, linguistic and other groups must be allowed to participate without discrimination in the government of their country, and that no part of the population can demand to govern alone.

There is very little if any support in international law for claims by separate ethnic, linguistic or religious groups inside sovereign States to secede from the territory of the sovereign States. Such claims are generally held to be invalid except under extreme circumstances. This is so also when the ethnic group claiming the right calls itself a 'nation', a 'people' or something else.

There is, however, some support for claims made by *indigenous peoples* for a right to some form of autonomy within sovereign States. The scope and modalities, however, remain vague, and its substance will be clarified only by further discussion in the context of international law.

In recent years, some support has emerged for the right of other ethnic, religious or linguistic groups under some circumstances to gain a degree of autonomy if that is necessary to enable them to preserve their identity and ensure effective political participation within the national society as a whole. The scope and nature of such a right remains vague and needs to be developed through future practice.

The Vienna 1993 Declaration and Programme of Action Article 2[8] deals with self-determination. The Conference recognizes and endorses the right of all peoples to self-determination. However, the principle of territorial integrity and political unity of existing, sovereign and independent States excludes a right to secession. This is reconfirmed by the Vienna Declaration. While this corresponds to the prevailing understanding in existing international law, the restatement made in Vienna helped to remove some controversies which had recently arisen.

We shall now take a closer look at the different components of the Vienna provisions, taking into account that they are derived from earlier sources of international law. Article 2, para 1:

> All peoples have the right of self-determination. By virtue of that right they freely determine their political status, and freely pursue their economic, social and cultural development.

This is a verbatim restatement of Article 1 para.1 of the 1966 Covenant of Human Rights, and leaves open all the ambiguities of that Article: who are the people (the self)? And what does the people have a right to? To answer those questions, we must take a closer look at the two other parts of the Vienna Declaration Article 2, para 2:

> Taking into account the particular situation of peoples under colonial or other forms of alien domination or foreign occupation, the World Conference on Human Rights recognizes the right of peoples to take any legitimate action, in accordance with the Charter of the United Nations, to realize their inalienable right of self-determination. The World Conference on Human Rights considers the denial of self-determination as a violation of human rights and underlines the importance of the effective realization of this right.

By 'the people' in the quotation above is meant the population as a whole, living in a non-self-governing territory or in an occupied territory. The 'people' is defined by the territory in which the population lives, not by the ethnicity, language or religion of the different groups which constitute the population. This becomes clear when looking at United Nations practice, which will be considered at greater length below.

The right of a population living in a non-self-governing territory to 'freely determine its political status, and freely pursue its economic, social and cultural development' is readily understandable. What it means has been further clarified in practice through the efforts by the United Nations to ensure that non-self-governing territories reach a status of sovereignty, separately or in other ways. This will be discussed below. Article 2, para 3:

> In accordance with the 1970 Declaration on Principles of International Law Concerning Friendly Relations and Cooperation Among States in Accordance with the Charter of the United Nations, this[9] shall not be construed as authorizing or encouraging any action which would dismember or impair, totally or in part, the territorial integrity or political unity of sovereign and independent States conducting themselves in compliance with the principle of equal rights and self-determination of peoples and thus possessed of a government representing the whole people belonging to the territory without distinction of any kind.

This provision excludes the use of the right to self-determination as a basis for secession except in very special circumstances. The same point had already been expressed in the 1962 Declaration on Decolonization,[10] operative Article 6:

> Any attempt aimed at the partial or total disruption of the national unity and the territorial integrity of a country is incompatible with the purposes and principles of the Charter of the United Nations.

However, the 1993 Vienna formulation adds that the government shall conduct itself in compliance with the principle of equal rights and self-determination of peoples by being possessed of a government representing the whole people belonging to the territory without distinction of any kind. The Vienna formulation therefore does not imply that the people of an independent State does not have a right to self-determination. What it does mean is that their right to self-determination consists in a right to have an inclusive, representative and democratic government, which on behalf of the population as a whole freely can pursue the economic, social and cultural development of the country as a whole. The political status of the territory has already been settled by becoming a sovereign, independent State. The right to self-determination for the people (population) of a sovereign State is a right to democracy and respect for human rights.

3.5.1 TERRITORIAL CHANGE BY CONSENT

This is accepted under international law and is recognized by the United Nations and the OSCE. Several examples of recent practice can be mentioned here: the dissolution of the Union of Soviet Republics at the end of 1991, based on consent between the union republics, and the dissolution of Czechoslovakia into its two constituent republics. In such cases, the practice is to recognize the new States with the borders they had as union republics or provinces when they formed part of the wider federation. Similarly, the unification by consent of the two parts of Germany was in full harmony with international law.

Problems arise, however, concerning the determination of consent. In divided societies with strong cleavages in preferences concerning the future status of the territory, it has normally been determined by referenda. Such referenda are highly problematic, however, since they tend to polarize the society. In the worst cases, this can lead to violence from the losing side. Whenever possible, a change in the territorial arrangements should be preceded by a process ensuring full respect for human rights for all and parity of esteem between the groups, which persists after the change in territory has taken place.

3.5.2 THE TWO DIFFERENT CONTEXTS: THE FUNDAMENTAL DISTINCTION

Comparing paragraphs 2 and 3 quoted above from Article 2 of the Vienna Declaration and Programme of Action (1993), the basic distinction becomes apparent: there is, on the one hand, a right to self-determination for non-self-governing territories which includes a right to independence for the territory as a whole; on the other hand, there is a clear statement of non-applicability of that right as a basis for dismembering the territorial integrity of sovereign States, provided they have a government representing the whole people belonging to the territory of that sovereign State.

NON-SELF-GOVERNING TERRITORIES[11]

Here self-determination is territorially based. The 'people' is a composite body, comprising the total population of the non-self-governing territory. The boundaries of the territory are normally identical to the pre-independence administrative boundaries. As a general rule, this has been applied to processes of decolonization, particularly in Latin America and in Africa. It has been considered an overriding task not to allow territories to be torn apart between the different ethnic and religious groups, since this would lead to devastating violence.[12] It has also been applied to the territorial and frontier disputes arising from the dissolution of the former USSR and

Yugoslavia into their constituent republics: the United Nations and the CSCE quickly took the position that the territory of the newly independent States was the same as the territory of the union republics within the federation prior to dissolution.[13]

Under contemporary principles of international law as contained in the Charter of the United Nations, every populated territory throughout the world is expected to be or to become a sovereign and independent State or a part of a sovereign State; once it has so become, the main task for the international community is to protect its territorial integrity.

Since 1945 dependencies, colonies and occupied territories have been considered as anomalies under international law; their dependent status should be brought to an end by ensuring that every territory and its population enjoy or partake in full self-government. At the root of this is the UN Charter's Declaration Regarding Non-Self-Governing Territories (Articles 3 and 4). The principle has been further developed by the 1960 General Assembly Declaration on the granting of independence to colonial countries and peoples (GA res. 1514/XV). While that Declaration refers to 'independence', it has not been understood of necessity to require a separate, independent status for the territory; it can become part of a larger sovereign and independent State. The population itself might opt for several permissible forms of self-government. These options are outlined in General Assembly resolution 1541 (XV), Principle VI:

   (a) Emergence as a sovereign State;
   (b) Free association with an independent State;
   (c) Integration with an independent State.

The choice between these options belongs exclusively to the population of the territory concerned.[14]

It has been necessary to determine which territories are non-self-governing rather than integral parts of sovereign States. This was a major concern for the United Nations from 1960 onwards. Concretely, it was done by establishing criteria for the obligation of administering States to transmit information about non-self-governing territories. These criteria were elaborated in 1960 by General Assembly resolution 1541 (XV). Principle IV states:

Prima facie there is an obligation to transmit information in respect of a territory which is *geographically separate* and is *distinct ethnically and/or culturally* from the country administering it.

These are the criteria of separateness — 'geographically' and 'culturally'.

The other criterion concerns the nature of the relationship between the administering State and the people living in the territory. When that relationship is based on unequal rights, particularly in the political field, the presumption that it is a non-self-governing territory is increased.

Principle V of resolution 1541 (XV):

Once it has been established that such a *prima facie* case of geographical and ethnical or cultural distinctness of a territory exists, other elements may then be inter alia of an administrative, political, juridical, economic or historical nature. If they affect the relationship between the metropolitan State and the territory concerned in a manner which arbitrarily places the latter in a position or status of subordination, they support the presumption that there is an obligation to transmit information under Article 3e of the Charter.

In addition to geographical and cultural separateness, the other criterion is therefore subordination. In essence, it is a question of lack of democratic participation in the State as a whole. The characteristic feature of non-self-governing territories was that the population in those territories did not have an equal right to participate in the political life of the metropolitan territory.

The Decolonization Committee (Committee of 24) was set up under resolution 1514 (XV) which contained the Declaration on Decolonization. It has since drawn up a list of non-self-governing territories. The remaining non-self-governing territories by 1993 were: American Samoa, Anguilla, British Virgin Islands, Cayman Islands, East Timor, Falkland Islands (Malvinas), Gibraltar, Guam, Montserrat, New Caledonia, Pitcairn, St Helena, Tokelau, Turk and Caisco Islands, US Virgin Islands, and Western Sahara.

In the same category as the non-self-governing territories arising from colonial situations must be included territories which have been occupied by external armed forces, after the entry into force of the United Nations Charter and thus in violation of the Charter. Acquisition of territory by the use of force is, at least since 1945, illegal. Consequently, such territories must be placed on the same level as the traditional non-self-governing territories. While in the traditional colonial cases, the non-self-governing territory is usually remote from the administering State, in the case of the occupied territories these are often immediately bordering on the territory of the administering State.

In some cases, the population of a territory which is non-self-governing because of colonial subordination is not entitled to establish a new and independent State but has to accept incorporation into the surrounding State of which it is held to have legally been a part prior to colonization. These are the so-called 'colonial enclaves'. Colonial enclaves are tiny areas, detached by a colonial power from what was at the time of colonization a sovereign State or a pre-colonial entity comparable to a sovereign State. Examples in practice include Ifni (a tiny Spanish possession on the coast of Morocco), Sao Batista di Ajuda, French and Portuguese trading posts in India, and Macao which was a Portuguese trading post on the coast of China. More controversial has been the question whether Belize (in Honduras) and the Falkland Islands can be considered as colonial enclaves.

A separate category is constituted by territorial rights temporarily acquired under a treaty for example, the Panama Canal Zone, where territorial rights were held by the United States until 1977, based on a treaty related to the operation of the Canal. The territorial rights as such were brought to an end in 1977, but rights relating to the operation of the Canal were maintained. Another example is Hong Kong where the territory was leased by treaty by China to Britain for a period of ninety nine years from 1 July 1898. At the end of the lease, the territory reverts to China in July 1997.[15]

SELF-DETERMINATION OF POPULATIONS IN SOVEREIGN AND INDEPENDENT STATES

Independence freezes territory. As stated in the Vienna document there is no unilateral right under international law to secession by part of the territory of an independent State from its other parts, with a possible exception when the government is profoundly undemocratic and unrepresentative, a possibility to which we shall return later. The main and near-uncontested rule, however, is that secession is not a unilateral right under international law. The rule has solid justification also in human rights law, as will be discussed. All international organizations, not only the United Nations, but also the Council of Europe and the Organization for Security and Co-operation in Europe are built on the principle that territorial change of sovereign States shall not be brought about by force.

While it is not a *unilateral* right, territorial change is fully legitimate when it is based on the consent of the parties involved. Such change may be held to be particularly justified when the existing territorial arrangements were achieved in ways which would have been unacceptable under contemporary international law. As will be pointed out in the historical review in chapter 5, the right to self-determination did not become a part of general international law until well after the end of World War II. Its first explicit inclusion in international law was brought about by the adoption, in 1966, of the two main covenants on human rights and their common Article 1. Numerous territorial arrangements made in earlier times would, if they had been effected today, be seen as a violation of present-day international law. Since they already are in existence, however, they must be accepted until such time as there is consent to change. However, it is obviously legitimate to argue openly in favour of change and to seek to achieve the necessary consent to bring it about.

The right to self-determination does always exist as a right for the population of an independent and sovereign State as a whole: firstly, as a right to continue to remain independent and thus not be subjected to alien rule, and secondly as a right for the population to effectively govern itself, which means a right to a fully representative and democratic government.

THE CRUCIAL POINT: DEMOS VERSUS ETHNOS

From the above, it can be seen that the main function of self-determination in our time is to advance democracy. The population as a whole (the *demos*), not the separate ethnic groups (the *ethnoses*) with their different languages, religions and cultures and which together form the demos, should benefit from self-determination in the fullest sense of the word. It is generally destructive to physically separate the members of these groups, which over centuries have come to live more or less interspersed, many of whom have intermarried and given rise to new generations who have links with both cultures. This does not exclude the possibility that the different groups can find practical ways to ensure the protection of their separate identity and culture, and that this in some cases can take the form of cultural or territorial autonomy within the wider State. This will be further examined below.

3.6 THE RELEVANCE OF HUMAN RIGHTS AND MINORITY RIGHTS TO GROUP ACCOMMODATION

The international system of human rights imposes obligations on States to advance the emancipation of all their inhabitants, based on three principles: universality, equality, and respect for the individual. Every State has a dual task under international law: to participate at the international level in the promotion of the international rule of law, including the adoption of international measures to advance compliance with that law; and to implement, at the national level, those obligations contained in international law which are intended to ensure good governance and protection of human rights.

The principle of non-discrimination is most important, being fundamental to the whole human rights system. The importance of positive measures to restore or create equality where it did not exist in the past is closely related to this. At the same time, the State must respect and maintain conditions for pluralism.

In addition to the standard individual human rights, in recent years a body of international law relating to minorities has developed, which is of central importance to peaceful group accommodations. These will be examined in the next chapter.

4. HUMAN RIGHTS, MINORITIES, AND GROUP ACCOMMODATION

4.1 FOUNDATIONS OF HUMAN RIGHTS: FREEDOM AND EQUALITY

The ethical foundation of human rights is found in the Universal Declaration of Human Rights Article 1:

> All human beings are born free and equal in dignity and rights. They are endowed with reason and conscience and should act towards each other in a spirit of brotherhood.

International human rights law has developed almost explosively during recent decades, both globally[1] and at the regional level,[2] and now covers a wide field of human activity. The International Bill of Human Rights[3] covers civil, political, economic, social and cultural rights. Over the years, further and more detailed provisions have been adopted in such fields as the prevention of discrimination; the rights of women; the rights of the child; prevention of slavery, servitude and forced labour; human rights and the administration of justice; freedom of information; freedom of association; equality and non-discrimination in employment; human rights related to marriage, family and youth; social welfare, progress and development; the right to enjoy culture; human rights related to nationality, statelessness and asylum; prevention, prohibition and punishment of war crimes and crimes against humanity, including genocide, and humanitarian law in armed conflict. Were these rights safeguarded, peaceful group accommodation would be greatly facilitated.

The provisions on freedom of thought, conscience and religion (Universal Declaration Article 18), for instance, are relevant for minorities. Members of any religious group are entitled to manifest, in public as well as in private, their religion or belief in teaching, practice, worship and observance. Equally relevant is the right to freedom of opinion and expression (Universal Declaration Article 19), which includes the right to seek, receive and impart information and ideas through any media and regardless of frontiers. This right clearly includes the right to use one's mother tongue and to receive and to give information in that language; on this basis minority groups can assert their right to protect their own language. The right to freedom of peaceful assembly and association (Universal Declaration Article 20) is also relevant: minority groups are entitled to organize for the promotion of their interests and values by forming their own associations. Furthermore, everyone has the right to participate in the cultural life of the community (Universal Declaration Article 27). This implies, also, that members of minority groups can carry on their particular group culture.

The only limitations permissible in regard to these rights are those, determined by law, which have been set solely for the purpose of securing due recognition and respect for the rights and freedoms of others and of meeting the just requirements of morality, public order and the general welfare in a democratic society (Universal Declaration Article 29, para.2)

The catalogue of human rights listed in the Universal Declaration and in the numerous international human rights conventions which have been adopted since 1948 on its basis, are intended to ensure the freedom and equality of the individual, within the limits set by the need to live together in a democratic society. The rights of groups are subordinate to this basic principle. Neither majorities nor minorities can demand rights which violate the freedom and equality of the human being. Human rights exclude the right of majorities, as well as of minorities, to establish privileges for members of their group.

The significance of individual freedom, in regard to group accommodation, shall be examined later in this chapter. For the moment, we shall address the question of equality in dignity and rights. This principle is spelt out in numerous other provisions in international human rights law, starting with the Universal Declaration, Article 2, para. 1:

> Everyone is entitled to all the rights and freedoms set forth in this Declaration, without distinction of any kind, such as race, colour, sex, language, religion, political or other opinion, national or social origin, property, birth or other status.

Provisions on equality and non-discrimination are found in all major human rights instruments, universal and regional. The Universal Declaration Article 7 contains one of these provisions:

> All are equal before the law and are entitled without any discrimination to equal protection of the law. All are entitled to equal protection against any discrimination in violation of this Declaration and against any incitement to such discrimination.

The theme of equality occurs time and again, and is spelt out in the International Covenant on Civil and Political Rights Articles 2 and 26, the International Covenant on Economic, Social and Cultural Rights Article 2, the European Convention on Human Rights and Fundamental Freedoms Article 14, the Inter-American Convention Article 1, the African Charter on Human and Peoples' Rights Article 2.[4]

Within most societies, different cultures coexist, in the form of different religions, different languages, different ethnic groups or nationalities. This cultural coexistence, which is an unavoidable aspect of contemporary life, can easily generate discriminations in the form of exclusions, restrictions or preference. The main thrust of modern human rights is to counteract such tendencies. For that to happen, it has to be understood by everybody involved that while they adhere to separate linguistic traditions, have different national origins, or subscribe to different religions, they are all equal in dignity and rights and should act towards each other in a spirit of fraternity. Group conflicts arise when members of one or the other group do not accept the equality in dignity or rights of the members of other groups.

4.2 DOMESTIC IMPLEMENTATION OF INTERNATIONAL HUMAN RIGHTS LAW: MINIMUM OBLIGATIONS AND MORAL REQUIREMENTS

A large part of relevant human rights law is 'soft law'. It conveys only some minimum obligations which have to be respected, but in addition contains a number of *desiderata*, moral encouragement to take further steps. In many studies interpreting the various international instruments, the emphasis is on the content of the minimum obligations contained therein. The question implicitly posed is this: when would the State concerned be found to be in violation of international human rights law when failing to take certain measures? This, however, should be distinguished from what the State is entitled to do, in order to implement to the best of its ability a satisfactory accommodation of group relations.

It is in these circumstances that the Minority Declaration, as well as the Framework Convention of the Council of Europe, can serve as guides. The language contained in the provisions leaves the State a wide discretion, and there is no reason why that discretion should be interpreted in its minimalist sense. Thus, even where explicit obligations cannot be deduced from the text, measures can and should be adopted to the extent that they do not conflict with other aspects of human rights, in particular the rights of others.

4.3   OBLIGATIONS OF STATES

Members of the United Nations are generally obliged under the Charter to partici-pate in the protection and promotion of human rights.[5] By ratifying international human rights conventions, State parties undertake to respect and ensure the human rights contained in the convention concerned.[6]

Article 2 of the International Covenant on Civil and Political Rights reads, in part:

> Each State party to the present Covenant undertakes to *respect and to ensure* to all individuals within its territory and subject to its jurisdiction the rights recognized in the present Covenant, without distinction of any kind …

The State and its agents must abstain from violating the rights of individuals. But the State must also ensure those rights. The State must provide protection under the law in such a way that human rights can be enjoyed without threats from other, private parties. For this to be possible, there must exist a functioning legal order with legislative, administrative and judicial functions, including criminal law which can restrain individuals or groups from attacking each other.

The International Covenant on Economic and Social Rights provides in its corresponding Article 2 in part:

Each State party undertakes to take steps to the maximum of its available resources, with a view to achieving progressively the realization of the rights recognized in the present Covenant by all appropriate means, including particularly the adoption of legislative measures.

The obligation of States under the international human rights system is therefore threefold:

1. To *respect* the integrity and the freedom of individuals, in so far as that freedom is not used to deny the enjoyment of human rights by others.

2. To *protect* the freedom of action and the use of resources as against other, more assertive or aggressive subjects: protection of the right to life, to freedom from slavery and servitude, from violence and maltreatment by third parties; protection against more powerful economic interests which destroy the possibility of enjoying economic and social rights, protection against fraud, against unethical behaviour in trade and contractual relations, against the marketing and dumping of hazardous or dangerous products — to mention some examples from different fields.

3. To *fulfil* certain claims based on internationally recognized human rights, when these cannot otherwise be enjoyed. This may take two forms:

- assistance in order to provide *opportunities* for those who do not now have them;

- direct *provisions* of basic needs when no other possibility exists; for example; (a) in times of unemployment (such as during a recession); (b) for the disadvantaged, and the elderly; (c) during sudden situations of crisis or disaster; and (d) for those who are marginalized (for example due to structural transformations in the economy and production).[7]

The following description of desirable lines of action therefore reflects not only the minimal requirements, but also those measures which conform with the spirit of the international instruments in the field.

In divided societies, particular attention should be given to the obligation to ensure compliance with the law enforcement agencies with international human rights. Two major issues are of central importance: firstly, that law enforcement officials must be strictly impartial; secondly, that the use of force must be strictly limited.

Apart from the general human rights provisions which are binding on governments and therefore on all their agents, including law enforcement officials, special attention should be given to the Code of Conduct for Law Enforcement Officials, adopted by the United Nations General Assembly resolution 34/169, 12 December 1979. Under Article 2, law enforcement officials are required to respect and protect human dignity and maintain and uphold the human rights of all persons. In the commentary, the main instruments on human rights are referred to. It is therefore essential, inter alia, that law enforcement officials are strictly impartial in regard to race, national origin or ethnicity. Mention should also be made of the Basic Principles on the Use of Force and Firearms by Law Enforcement Officials, adopted by the United Nations Congress on the Prevention of Crime and the Treatment of Offenders, in 1990. It sets strict limits on the use of firearms. Intentional use of lethal arms can be permitted only when strictly unavoidable in order to protect life. The Principles also note that everyone is entitled to participate in lawful and peaceful demonstrations. In the policing of unlawful but non-violent demonstrations, law enforcement officials shall avoid the use of force or, when that is not practicable, restrict the use of force as much as possible. Even in the policing of violent and unlawful demonstrations law enforcement officials shall not intentionally use lethal weapons except when strictly unavoidable to protect life.

4.4 Implementing Equality in the Common Domain

Peaceful and constructive solutions to group accommodation and minority situations must start with effective measures to ensure equality and non-discrimination in the common domain within the national society.

One of the main instruments in international human rights law to counteract challenges to the equality of human beings is the International Covenant on the Elimination of All Forms of Racial Discrimination (ICERD).[8] The two objectives of ICERD are to eliminate racial discrimination in all its forms and to promote understanding among all races (Article 2, para. 1). Racial discrimination is defined in Article 1 as:

> Distinction, exclusion, restriction or preference based on race, colour, descent or *national or ethnic origin* which has the purpose or effect of nullifying or impairing the recognition, enjoyment or exercise, on an equal footing, of human rights and fundamental freedoms in the political, economic, social, cultural or any other field of public life.

It will be noted that 'racial discrimination' has a much broader meaning than the traditional, narrow understanding of 'race' in terms of genetic descent, the most visible aspect of which is colour. Racial discrimination also includes discrimination on the basis of national or ethnic origin; ethnicity, as we shall see later, is defined primarily by culture; consequently, racial discrimination includes discrimination based on the cultural origin or identity of the persons concerned. The aim is to achieve equality not only *de jure*, but also *de facto*. ICERD furthermore requires that special but transitional measures shall be taken in regard to racial or ethnic groups when this is required in order to guarantee to them full and equal enjoyment of human rights and fundamental freedoms.

The obligation to ensure equality implies that every State must ensure the existence of a common domain equally open to all, not directed and controlled by the demands, symbols or practices of any one ethnic group or one religion alone to the exclusion of others. In the common domain, every resident must be equally free to participate and to enjoy their human rights without being treated as a second class resident or citizen due to their ethnic, religious, linguistic or national background.

States have therefore undertaken to prohibit racial and ethnic segregation; to prohibit and punish acts of violence or incitement to such acts against any race or group of another colour or ethnic origin; to prohibit organizations which incite to racial and thereby also to ethnic discrimination and participation in such organizations.[9]

States have undertaken to guarantee the equal enjoyment by everyone of their rights in most aspects of their social, economic, political and cultural existence[10] namely, equal treatment before tribunals and other organs administering justice; equal right to security of person and protection by the State against violence or bodily harm, whether inflicted by government officials or by any individual group or institutions; equal political rights; equal civil rights;[11] equal enjoyment of economic, social and cultural rights,[12] which include the right to equal participation in cultural activities;[13]

and the right of equal access to any place or service intended for use by the general public.[14]

For this to be possible, however, a functioning democracy is required. The State must also respect the existence of and promote a vigorous civil society. Networks across ethnic groups, formed by associations and nongovernmental organizations of various kinds, are essential to withstand the destructive consequences of ethnic, linguistic or religious cleavages.

4.4.1 DOMESTIC LEGISLATION ON NON-DISCRIMINATION AND EQUALITY

Effective implementation at the national level of all provisions contained in ICERD would constitute a first line of defence against ethnic violence. Most States recognize their responsibility for ensuring equality and non-discrimination within their territory. This is reflected in the number of States which have ratified and therefore become parties to ICERD,[15] higher than for any other human rights convention, with the exception of the International Convention on the Rights of the Child (ICRC).

Most States have adopted national legislation covering many or all of the provisions of ICERD, and thereby seek to ensure equality in different fields of national law.[16] The overwhelming majority of States recognize that individuals are entitled to equality of treatment before the law, and most States have introduced this principle into their constitution or passed legislation to this effect.

4.4.2 ENJOYMENT OF CIVIL RIGHTS WITHOUT DISCRIMINATION

Many States have explicitly recognized the need to ensure that civil rights are enjoyed by all without discrimination.

The right to security of the person must be guaranteed by the State to all persons, citizens and non-citizens alike, irrespective of ethnic, linguistic and religious background. Many countries have adopted legislation to guarantee non-discrimination in this field.[17]

Equality and non-discrimination in the exercise of political rights is also implicit or explicit in the legislation of most countries. The purpose is to bar the possibility of ethnic or racial discrimination in political life. In some countries this is explicitly stated,[18] but in other cases it is implicit in the general principle of equal and universal suffrage which is contained in many constitutions.

Freedom of association and the right to assembly are provided for, in many countries, without distinction of race, which again includes distinctions on the grounds of ethnicity.

Most countries have national legislation prohibiting discrimination in employment, in access to housing, in access to education, and to public services and facilities.

ICERD Article 4 (b) obliges States to prohibit organizations and organized propaganda activities which promote and incite racial (and thereby also ethnic or national) discrimination, and makes participation in such organizations punishable by law.

While an increasing number of States emphasize in their legislation everyone's freedom of expression, steps are also taken to prohibit the use of freedom of expression to promote racism, xenophobia and racial and ethnic hatred. This entails dilemmas; while the prevention of incitement to hatred is essential, the prohibition can sometimes be used selectively as an instrument to block the right of minorities to articulate the discrimination to which they are subjected, without comparable enforcement directed against violations by majority members. The problem of bias among law enforcement agencies constitutes a serious obstacle.

Of special importance, therefore, in light of contemporary ethnic conflicts, are the provisions on the prohibition of racial or ethnic hatred or xenophobia. Many States have incorporated such legislation. Its effectiveness depends on several factors: that it is generally adhered to by the public; that it is applied consistently and impartially by the courts, and that it is enforced without any bias by the police and security forces. The first line to crumble is often the local police. It is frequently reported that local police forces are affected by stereotypes and prejudices and therefore do not manage to behave impartially and to protect the vulnerable groups against attack. When conflicts become more severe, the local police are sometimes pushed aside by militants who take the law into their own hands.

When security forces seek to repress an ethnic challenge, they often overreact and resort to indiscriminate action affecting civilians and non-combatants, leading to strengthened resistance and more indiscriminate action on the other side. From then on there is often a negative spiral of violations and counter-violations leading to an escalation where the legal machinery gradually loses power, at its worst ending in a period of near-anarchy or protracted conflict with intransigence on both sides.

It is therefore of primary importance for States which want to ensure peaceful and constructive solutions to situations involving minorities to prepare the police and the security forces for their difficult task of impartial and effective response to any form of ethnic discrimination, wherever it originates. In some cases, members of the minority group are attacked by death squads or assassinated, and the police or security forces fail to search and to prosecute those who have committed the act. The feeling, among members of the minority, of a lack of equal protection of personal security by the law, is a major factor in the hardening of attitudes.

Manifestations of ethnic and racial prejudice are still widespread, even where the law enforcement officials seek to act against it.

4.4.3 NATIONAL INSTITUTIONS FOR ETHNIC AND RACIAL HARMONY

Fortunately, a wide range of measures have been taken in many countries to counteract the spread of racial and ethnic violence. States have established institutions such as commissions on racial equality, human rights commissions, ombudsman institutions, in one case (Sweden) a separate Ethnic Discrimination Ombudsman, minority councils, and numerous other mechanisms.

4.4.4 AFFIRMATIVE ACTION

Inter-ethnic conflicts may be more manageable when disparities in income and development between the groups are reduced.

Affirmative action is one way to advance equality in the enjoyment of human rights within societies where there has been in the past systemic discrimination, whether social or political. It implies the use of preferential measures and might therefore appear to be in conflict with the principle of non-discrimination. Under international human rights law, preferential measures are permissible under certain circumstances. This has been made clear in ICERD Article 1(4) and Article 2(2). Affirmative action is preference, by way of special measures, for certain groups or members of such groups (typically defined by race, ethnic identity, or sex) to secure adequate advancement of such groups or their individual members in order to ensure equal enjoyment of human rights and fundamental freedoms.

Such measures cannot be continued, however, after the purpose has been achieved. When the equal enjoyment, across racial, ethnic or sex lines, of human rights, has been achieved, continued preference for members of the previously discriminated-against group would constitute unjustified discrimination since it would from then on lead to the unequal enjoyment of human rights. It is stated as follows in ICERD Article 1, para. 4 *in fine*:

> … provided, however, that such measures do not, as a consequence, lead to the maintenance of separate rights for different racial groups and that they shall not be continued after the object for which they were taken has been achieved.

Affirmative action is therefore intended to create equality, but is different both from non-discrimination and from targeted support to individuals based on their individual need to obtain equality of opportunity.

There are 'soft' and 'hard' versions of affirmative action. The 'soft' versions are extensions of the principle of non-discrimination and are intended to deal with latent social discrimination creating obstacles to members of groups affected by such discrimination. In evaluating the claims made by the group or its members there is a requirement that some preference be given in order to offset the effects of such latent discriminatory attitudes.

Stronger versions of affirmative action are aimed at an accelerated creation of a balanced society, one where there is equality in participation at all levels, in political life, in professions, in the economy and in other fields. Typical of this is the establishment of quotas for access to education at higher levels, to civil service, to professions, and in employment. Such approaches to affirmative action suspend or modify traditional criteria of merit as a basis of access, but can be justified when there were, in the past, discriminatory practices which deprived members of those groups of equal opportunity and blocked them from the application of criteria of merit.

The sociopolitical context has to be taken into account. Different societies, with very different social, ethnic and political conditions, can justifiably place their emphasis on different approaches. The main concern should be to reach the goal, which is equality in the enjoyment of human rights; how it is to be done depends on pre-existing conditions of inequality and other factors to be taken into account.

4.4.5 REALIZATION OF ECONOMIC AND SOCIAL RIGHTS

Affirmative action for members of a group previously discriminated against through preferential treatment can generate serious resentment among members of the other ethnic groups, and thereby intensify rather than reduce ethnic tension.

Another approach to the restoration of equality is to implement, without discrimination and based on need rather than ethnicity, the economic, social and cultural rights which form an integral part of the contemporary international human rights system.

The industrial and post-industrial societies have developed their own particular solutions. The basis of the welfare States in Western and Northern Europe, and to some extent in other parts of the world, is a free market economy, combined with the transfer of some part of the product, through direct and indirect taxation, to ensure equal opportunities for all and to ensure that the fundamental necessities (health services, basic social security) are enjoyed by everyone, irrespective of their income and social position. There are also constraints on over-aggressive processes of private capital accumulation. These constraints have been achieved by social reform movements made possible through wide and pluralist political participation, and reinforced by the growing acceptance of economic and social rights as part of the human rights system. The functioning of free trade unions has been essential in this connection.

The outcome therefore has been a focus on protection or creation of equal opportunity through targeted support for those who, for whatever reason, did not have an equal starting base for participation in the economic and social life of society, combined with a social safety net for those who, for whatever reason, still fail to secure their needs through their own endeavours.

4.5 THE RIGHTS OF (PERSONS BELONGING TO) MINORITIES

The search for multicultural pluralism combines efforts to ensure equal opportunity for everyone in the national society with programmes to allocate resources, power and space for separate groups. It requires tolerance and encouragement of ethnic political parties as part of the political system, in order that the different communal groups can participate in power-sharing or at least have an impact on decision-making, yet it also requires brokerage of cross-ethnic or cross-religious alliances concerned with issues other than ethnicity or religion.

Article 27 of the International Covenant on Civil and Political Rights provides that:

> In those States in which ethnic, religious or linguistic minorities exist, persons belonging to such minorities shall not be denied the right, in community with the other members of their group, to enjoy their own culture, to profess and practice their own religion, or to use their own language.

This Article remains the main provision, in conventional[19] international law, on the rights of minorities. It is individualistic in its orientation (the beneficiaries are not minority groups but 'persons belonging to'). Nevertheless, it has been interpreted to establish too a platform, however modest, for group claims. There is extensive literature on the interpretation and scope of Article 27.[20] The United Nations Human Rights Committee has developed its interpretation in a number of specific cases.[21]

The Declaration on the Rights of National or Ethnic, Religious and Linguistic Minorities (hereinafter called the Minority Declaration), adopted by consensus by the General Assembly on 18 December 1992, is at present the main guide to evaluating State practice.[22] It is not in itself legally binding; it is, however, inspired by, or builds on, existing international law and relevant international documents: on ICCPR Article 27; on provisions in ICERD Article 2.2; in the UNESCO convention against discrimination in education; in the ILO convention 169 concerning Indigenous and Tribal Peoples in Independent Countries; on several provisions in the draft Universal Declaration on the Rights of Indigenous Peoples; on the CSCE[23] documents, including in particular the Copenhagen document of 1991; on the African Charter on Human and Peoples' Rights (which refers to peoples, not minorities).

Article 1 of the Minority Declaration calls on States to protect the existence and identity of minorities and to encourage conditions for the enjoyment of that identity. The same Article further provides that the existence and the national or ethnic, cultural, religious and linguistic identity of minorities shall be protected by States within their territories, and that States shall encourage conditions for the promotion of that identity.

This declaration has now become the most important international text on group accommodation. Being so new, its impact on State behaviour remains to be seen.

It represents a clear trend in international law towards greater recognition of the multicultural composition of national societies. This is reflected in Article 2:

> Persons belonging to national or ethnic, religious and linguistic minorities (hereinafter referred to as persons belonging to minorities) have the right to enjoy their own culture, to profess and practice their own religion, and to use their own language, in private and in public, freely and without interference or any form of discrimination.

> Persons belonging to minorities have the right to participate effectively in cultural, religious, social, economic and public life.

Under Article 4, para. 2 of the Declaration:

> States shall take measures to create favourable conditions to enable persons belonging to minorities to express their characteristics and to develop their culture, language, religion, traditions and customs, except where specific practices are in violation of national law and contrary to international standards.

States, therefore, are under an obligation to take positive measures of special protection for minorities, in order for them to develop their culture, language and religion.

4.5.2 STANDARD-SETTING BY THE OSCE

The Organization for Security and Co-operation in Europe (until 1994: CSCE[24])has since 1990 taken a strong interest in the protection of minorities.[25] The most important event in this respect was the CSCE Copenhagen Meeting of the Conference on the Human Dimension, June 1990.[26] The Concluding Document of the Copenhagen meeting has elaborate provisions, many of which have inspired the United Nations Declaration. Elements of the Copenhagen Concluding Document are given below:

(32) Persons belonging to national minorities have the right freely to express, preserve and develop their ethnic, cultural, linguistic or religious identity and to maintain and develop their culture in all its aspects, free of any attempts at assimilation against their will. In particular, they have the right

(32.1) to use freely their mother tongue in private as well as in public;

(32.2) to establish and maintain their own educational, cultural and religious institutions, organizations or associations, which can seek voluntary financial and other contributions as well as public assistance, in conformity with national legislation.

(32.3) to profess and practise their religion, including the acquisition, possession and use of religious materials, and to conduct religious educational activities in their mother tongue;

(33.4) to establish and maintain unimpeded contacts among themselves within their country as well as contacts across frontiers with citizens of other States with whom they share a common ethnic or national origin, cultural heritage or religious beliefs;

(32.5) to disseminate, have access to and exchange information in their mother tongue;

(32.6) to establish and maintain organizations or associations within their country and to participate in international non-governmental organizations. Persons belonging to national minorities can exercise and enjoy their rights individually as well as in community with other members of their group. No disadvantage may arise for a person belonging to a national minority on account of the exercise or non-exercise of any such rights.

(33) The participating States will protect the ethnic, cultural, linguistic and religious identity of national minorities on their territory and create conditions for the promotion of that identity. They will take the necessary measures to that effect after due consultations, including contacts with organizations or associations of such minorities, in accordance with the decision-making procedures of each State. Any such measures

will be in conformity with the principles of equality and non-discrimination with respect to the other citizens of the participating State concerned.

(34) The participating States will endeavour to ensure that persons belonging to national minorities, notwithstanding the need to learn the official language or languages of the State concerned, have adequate opportunities for instruction of their mother tongue or in their mother tongue, as well as, wherever possible and necessary, for its use before public authorities, in conformity with applicable national legislation. In the context of the teaching of history and culture in educational establishments, they will also take account of the history and culture of national minorities.

(35) The participating States will respect the right of persons belonging to national minorities to effective participation in public affairs, including participation in the affairs relating to the protection and promotion of the identity of such minorities.

4.5.2 STANDARD-SETTING BY THE COUNCIL OF EUROPE

The Council of Europe has established what is the most effective contemporary international instrument ensuring compliance with human rights. A primary aspect of the Council of Europe is to secure democracy, which among other things emphasizes the rights of the *demos* (the whole population of a country) and therefore emphasizes inclusiveness, rather than the *ethnos*, which might lead to discrimination and separateness rather than to the safeguarding of human rights.

The European Convention for the Protection of Human Rights and Fundamental Freedoms provides in Article 14 that:

> The enjoyment of the rights and freedoms set forth in this Convention shall be secured without discrimination on any ground such as … association with a national minority.

A rich case law has developed within the Council of Europe protecting members of minorities from discrimination in areas such as freedom of expression and association, the freedom to use the language of their own choice and to communicate thoughts and opinions in whatever language they wish.

Against the background of European history, however, there has been considerable reluctance to encourage the evolution of group rights under the European system.

Nevertheless, the concern with rights of members of national and other minorities has surfaced on numerous occasions. In 1992, the Council adopted the European Charter on Regional and Minority Languages. It calls for measures to facilitate the use of minority languages in regard to education, in the conduct of judicial proceedings, relations with public authorities, and access to the mass media, and the fostering of cultural, economic and social activities. It also aims at the facilitation, for these purposes, of transfrontier contacts and exchange.[27]

In November 1994 the Council of Europe adopted the Framework Convention on Minorities. The Convention is significant for two reasons. It is the first multilateral 'hard law' instrument devoted in its entirety to the protection of minorities, and it contains much more detailed provisions on such protection than any other international instrument. It is 'hard law' in the sense that it constitutes legally binding obligations for States which ratify the Convention.

That said, several limitations must also be noted. The Convention contains mostly programme-type provisions, which means that it contains objectives to be pursued by the ratifying State, but its provisions are not directly applicable in national law. The objectives leave wide discretion to States in the implementation of the objectives. The Convention does not recognize collective rights, but emphasizes the rights of persons belonging to national minorities — rights which they can, however, exercise alone or in association with others.

The European Framework Convention contains the most detailed guidelines yet adopted for the accommodation of groups within sovereign States, building as it does on the United Nations Minority Declaration and on the Copenhagen Document of the CSCE (now OSCE). Some of its elements, therefore, will be briefly outlined below.

The Convention emphasizes respect for the principles of international law in Article 2 with its implicit reference to the United Nations General Assembly resolution 2625 (XXV), containing the Declaration on Principles of International Law Concerning Friendly Relations and Cooperation Among States in accordance with the Charter of the United Nations, and in Article 21 which underlines that nothing in the Convention can be interpreted to imply a right to engage in any activity contrary to principles of international law and in particular against the sovereign equality, territorial integrity and political independence of States.

The Framework Convention on Minorities of the Council of Europe therefore consolidates a principle basic to all international instruments in this field: group accommodation must be effected within the limits of existing territorial integrity of States unless all parties agree to a voluntary territorial change.

It starts with the principle of equality in the common domain (Article 4, in particular para. 2). It continues by obliging States to promote conditions necessary for persons belonging to national minorities to maintain and develop their culture, and to preserve the essential elements of their identity, namely their religion, traditions, and cultural heritage.

The Convention calls on the parties to encourage a spirit of tolerance and inter-cultural dialogue and to take measures to protect persons, whether belonging to minorities or majorities, who may be subject to threats of acts of discrimination, hostility or violence as a result of their ethnic, cultural, linguistic or religious identity (Article 6). Article 9 provides for the freedom of expression and information of members of minorities, including access to media for persons belonging to minorities, allowing for cultural pluralism.

Article 10 deals with the use by members of minorities of their language, including its use in regard to administrative authorities in areas where many members of the minorities live. Article 11 provides for the right to use one's own name in the form it has in the minority language and to have it officially recognized, the right to display signs in the minority language, and the use of traditional local names, street names and other topographical indications when there is sufficient demand for such indications.

Article 12 requires States to take measures in the fields of education and research to foster knowledge of the culture, history, language and religion of the national minorities and of the majority. Under Article 13, members of national minorities have the right to set up and manage their own private educational and training establishment, but this shall not entail financial obligations for the States.

Under Article 14, States undertake to recognize the right of persons belonging to minorities to learn their minority language, and to provide opportunities for being taught the minority language or for receiving instruction in that language. This shall be done without prejudice to the learning of the official language of the country concerned. Under Article 15, conditions shall be created for the effective participation of persons belonging to national minorities in cultural, social and economic life and in public affairs, in particular those affecting them.

Article 16 requires States to refrain from measures altering the proportions of the population in areas inhabited by persons belonging to national minorities when such measures are aimed at restricting the rights and freedoms contained in the Convention. Under Article 17 the States undertake not to interfere with the rights of persons belonging to national minorities to establish contacts across frontiers with persons living in other States, particularly with those with whom they share an ethnic, cultural, linguistic or religious identity.

Article 18 calls on States to conclude bilateral and multilateral agreements with other States, in particular neighbouring States, in order to ensure the protection of persons belonging to the national minorities concerned. This relates to the effort to create stability between home State and kin State, which is further dealt with in chapter 5 of the present study, where the elaboration of the 'Stability Pact' adopted in March 1995 on the initiative of the French Prime Minister Balladur is also discussed.

Under Article 19 of the Framework Convention, the States parties undertake to implement the principles in the Convention with only such limitations as are provided for in international legal instruments, in particular the European Convention for the Protection of Human Rights and Fundamental Freedoms. Conversely, in Article 20, persons belonging to a national minority shall respect the national legislation and the rights of others, in particular those of persons belonging to the majority or other national minorities. These two Articles must therefore be read in conjunction: while minorities must respect national law (Article 20), such law should contain no other limitations on the rights recognized in the Convention than those which follow from international human rights law and other parts of international law (Article 19).

The international monitoring of the implementation of the Convention by the States parties is to be undertaken by the Committee of Ministers of the Council of Europe, under Article 24, but the Committee shall make use of an advisory committee composed of recognized experts in the field of the protection of national minorities.

4.6 IMPLEMENTING MINORITY RIGHTS

4.6.1 PROTECTING THE EXISTENCE OF MINORITIES: THE RELEVANCE OF NATIONAL RECOGNITION

The existence of minor and major groups in society is a matter of fact. It does not depend on any formal act of recognition of a specific minority, be it by a bilateral treaty or by national law. Bilateral treaties may, due to relations between two States and often as a consequence of a peace settlement, single out a particular group for protection. However, members of all groups which fulfil the necessary criteria are entitled to the protection provided for under general international law, when members of the group want to maintain and develop their common characteristics which are different from those of the majority.

While no formal recognition is required for the group to exist, States are called upon under Article 1 of the Minority Declaration to take the necessary legislative measures to protect their existence and identity and to encourage conditions for the promotion of that identity. In doing so, States may consider it necessary to mention the specific groups which are the intended beneficiaries of the legislation. There is a danger that such legislation could exclude some groups. It can be avoided by referring to abstract criteria for the existence of minorities, rather than by naming them.

4.6.2 IDENTITY

The cultural and spiritual dimensions of existence are also fundamental to the Declaration. Therefore, their identity is to be protected and conditions for its promotion to be encouraged. In the past, minority groups were sometimes effectively denied their existence through policies of forced assimilation or ethnocide. It is now generally recognized, in line with the evolution within UNESCO on these matters, that each culture has a dignity and value which must be respected and preserved, to the extent compatible with universal human rights.[28]

Several identity provisions are now found in international instruments. These include provisions in favour of children (Articles 29 and 30 of the Convention on the Rights of the Child), migrant workers (Article 31 of the UN Migrant Workers

Convention); indigenous peoples (Article 2 (2) (b) of ILO Convention No. 169, which refers to respect for 'their social and cultural identity, their customs and traditions and their institutions'),or just 'human beings' (Article 1.3 of the UNESCO Declaration on Race and Racial Prejudice). Cultural and other identities are also referred to in the CSCE instruments, including the Copenhagen Human Dimensions Conference and the CSCE Geneva Meeting of Experts on National Minorities of 1991.

4.6.3 INFORMATION AND EXPRESSION: FREEDOM AND ACCESS

Information freedoms are essential, including freedom of expression, the right to impart information in the minority language, right to access to public media, and the right of the minority through its own mass media. The right to freedom of expression is a general human right, and it includes the right to receive and to impart information and ideas in the minority language without interference by public authorities and regardless of frontiers. This is general international human rights law; more importantly, it also encompasses a right to access without discrimination to the State-owned media as well as the right to use one's own means of communication. This should allow a minority the same right as a majority to take up any issue, not only specific cultural issues related to the minority, but also political considerations, limited only by such general rules as limit the rights of minorities and others to bring up political issues.[29] The members of minorities must be able, in their own language, to address their own constituency on general public issues of significance for society as a whole and therefore also for them.

4.6.4 RIGHT TO USE OWN LANGUAGE IN CONTACTS WITH AUTHORITIES AND COURTS

The question of the language to be used in contacts with national authorities and the courts constitutes one of the most essential questions for members of minorities. Two problems are involved: due process, and preservation of identity. Due process, particularly in the case of criminal cases before the courts, makes it essential that those accused are able to address the court in a language in which they are fully fluent. This is part of ordinary, individual human rights. The International Covenant on Civil and Political Rights Article 14, para. 3 states:

> In the determination of any criminal charge against him, everyone shall be entitled to the following minimum guarantees, in full equality: … (f) to have the free assistance of an interpreter if he cannot understand or speak the language used in court.

However, should the person concerned be sufficiently fluent in the official language of the country concerned, this provision does not help. It has not been adopted in order to ensure identity, but due process.

For members of minorities, however, it is important to be able to address the court and other authorities in their own language, in order to feel secure that their own language is sufficient to be able to function in society, and thus to be at ease in the preservation of one's identity. In practice, it is generally accepted that minorities can use their own language in regard to courts and authorities within territorial units of the State in which that minority language is prominent or is very widely used.[30]

4.6.5 PRESERVATION AND DEVELOPMENT OF MINORITY CULTURE

Culture includes the cultural environment, including street names and toponyms. Under the Framework Convention for the Protection of National Minorities of the Council of Europe, Article 11(3), States shall endeavour '… to display traditional local names, street names and other topographical indications intended for the public also in the minority language where there is a sufficient demand for such indications.'

In Finland, the largest minority group consists of the Swedish-speaking Finnish citizens. A sophisticated system of bilingualism is in force, affecting education at all levels including universities, toponyms and street names, as well as the use of own language in public, in relations with the authorities, and in government institutions.

The Constitution of Sweden provides for the promotion of opportunities for ethnic, linguistic and religious minorities to maintain and develop a cultural and community life of their own. Special provisions have been made for the education of the Sami population. Religious communities may receive funding to help finance their religious activities and to help pay for their premises.[31]

The Romanian Constitution, Article 6(1) recognizes and guarantees members of national minorities the right to preserve, develop and express their ethnic, cultural, linguistic and religious identity. With regard to culture, it may be noted that cultural and artistic institutions for members of national minorities are financed by the State. Religious minorities have their own churches. The State guarantees freedom of religious education, in accordance with the needs of each denomination.[32] In Spain the use of the various languages spoken apart from Spanish (Castilian) has also been strengthened in recent years. Catalan, Galician, Mallorcan, Valencian and Basque are official languages together with Spanish. The relevant languages are used in education, administration, literature, the theatre and cinema, and television and radio.[33]

Norway, which for at least a century pursued a policy of assimilation adversely affecting its indigenous people, the Sami, has reversed its policy during the last two decades. A new Article 110 was inserted into the Constitution on 27 May 1988: 'It is the responsibility of the authorities of the State to create conditions enabling the Sami people to preserve and develop its language, culture and way of life.' A Sami Assembly or Parliament (Sametinget) was established by law of 12 June 1987, and started work in October 1989. Under additional legislation the Sami people have been given extensive language rights, in education and in communication with local public bodies. Six municipalities in northern Norway form an administrative area for the Sami language.

4.6.6 EDUCATION IN MULTICULTURAL SOCIETIES

States should take measures in the field of education, in order to encourage knowledge of the history, traditions, language and culture of the national minorities existing within that territory. Persons belonging to such minorities should have adequate opportunities to gain knowledge of their society as a whole.

One point only will be added here. The issue of the content of education is essential both for the preservation of minority identity, and for familiarization with the common values of the national society. It is a very controversial issue but the Convention on the Rights of the Child, Article 29, which spells out the threefold requirement for education offers guidance. States parties to the Convention agree that the education of the child shall be directed to:

> (c) the development of respect for the child's parents, his or her own cultural identity, for the national values of the country in which the child is living, the country from which he or she may originate and for civilizations different from his or her own.

75

The following is also important:

> (d) The preparation of the child for responsible life in a free society, in the spirit of understanding, peace, tolerance, equality of sexes, and friendship among all peoples, ethnic, national and religious groups and persons of indigenous origins.

4.6.7 EFFECTIVE POLITICAL PARTICIPATION AND CROSS-ETHNIC CONSENSUS ARRANGEMENTS

Human rights require that everyone within the nation shall have the same rights to political representation. In societies deeply divided by ethnic, religious or linguistic affiliations, this is not a simple matter. Two requirements should be fulfilled: one, that the political system should ensure peaceful group accommodation; two, that each of the groups can be ensured respect for their identity and their justified interests.

Pure majoritarian governance in divided societies constitutes a serious threat to group accommodation. This is now widely recognized. Two options, or a combination, can help: (a) consociational democracy, including electoral systems which create ongoing incentives for inter-ethnic cooperation, and (b) in some cases territorial subdivision through federal systems or autonomies.[34]

The notion of consociational democracy, introduced by Arent Lijphart,[35] has been used to describe a form of power-sharing through a multiple balance of power among the segments of a plural society which allow for decision-making by the 'grand coalition method'. It is seen as an alternative to the majoritarian type of democracy, and more suitable for good government in plural societies divided by ethnic, linguistic, religious or cultural differences, where the groups are clearly identifiable.

Consociational democracy can take many forms. It is typically built on principles of power-sharing both at the executive and the legislative level, making use of proportional representation and various arrangements for weighted voting, with a degree of self-administration for each group, whether they live together or separately. In several of its forms it involves risks also, as shown by several critics, including Kumar Rupesinghe.[36] Some of its forms tend to freeze ethnic identities and lead to long-term polarization. Another expert in the field, Crawford Young, in a recent summary report for the United Nations Research Institute for Social Development (UNRISD) has summed up some of the experiences of different countries.[37] He observes that when cultural difference is the central organizing principle of political life, consociationalism produces a complete ethnic corporatizing of society, which might not be desirable for those to whom concerns other than national or ethnic identity are also of high importance. Formal consociationalism would make it necessary to fix the units of identity permanently or for long periods of time.

There are many arrangements, however, which, while not constituting power-sharing in the formal sense of the word, lead to a necessity in practice for the different groups to cooperate if they are to make any necessary decisions. The important task is to find a mix which does not entirely block decision-making but which encourages cooperation across the divided segments of society. The idea of power-sharing can be made more flexible, to refer in more general terms to the quest for balanced representation in national institutions.

Appropriate electoral systems are crucial in this regard. It is essential, in the further debate regarding Northern Ireland and a possible future, agreed united Ireland, that voting and representation are given close attention. It has not been possible in this paper to address this important issue in detail. Only a few observations will be made here.

Numerous alternatives can be found when practices in different countries are examined. In divided societies, preference must be given to electoral systems which provide incentives for accommodative practices rather than to those which mobilize political support for ethnic extremism. The system should encourage such accommodation in the run up to elections, rather than through bargaining between the groups after representatives have been elected on purely ethnic or communal grounds.

Experimentation in this domain is a tempting policy approach because the choice of electoral system has a significant effect on structuring representation in a diverse society, and because it is easier to accomplish adjustments incrementally in electoral systems than to achieve more fundamental reconfigurations of constitutional State structures. Electoral systems are 'the most easily manipulable feature of a political system', according to Young.

He notes that most of continental Europe has opted for proportional representation formulas, in contrast to single-member districts with plurality voting, while systems modelled upon Anglo-American practice employ variations on the first-past-the-post plurality formulas. He also notes that the 'Westminster model' plurality system has undoubtedly lost standing. There are many cultural circumstances where its impact is perverse; he observes that Northern Ireland (where it has been abandoned for local elections, but not for elections to the British Parliament) is an obvious case. If communal voting patterns predominate, and the party system is rooted in cultural segments, its tendency to overrepresent majorities and to underrepresent minorities is a major shortcoming.

Proportional representation (PR) can use either a national constituency, or a number of multi-member districts. Seats are attributed according to the proportion of votes received, with diverse formulas of calculation available, including the 'topping up' of representatives of parties which would otherwise have been underrepresented within the national constituency as a whole.

PR has the obvious merit that it can reflect political demographics in elected institutions, including ethnicity, if this shapes voting behaviour and party nomination strategy, but it also encourages cross-ethnic political alignments, which stimulates bargaining and consensus-seeking.

Proportional arrangements can also be introduced within the political parties. Ideally, political institutions should be structured in such a way that it would be in the interest of political parties to have support from persons belonging to both (all) ethnic or religious groups in order to be elected.

Various forms of quotas could be added to proportional representation within the decision-making bodies as well as within the parties. One type of quota used in some countries, formally or informally, seeks to ensure egalitarian gender representation by requiring that at least a third or more of the candidates for election shall be women.

In constructive power-sharing arrangements, mechanisms are arranged to prevent undesirable blocking of the decision-making in the executive body or in the legislature through the use of veto by one of the groups. However, one of the express purposes of power-sharing is to block decisions which are clearly inimical to one of the main groups in society. The other purpose, nevertheless, is to have a continuous framework of negotiation at the highest political level, so that all matters of practical importance can be handled through cooperation and bargaining. Much depends on the democratic political culture; formal arrangements alone cannot solve all problems in a divided society.

It should normally be possible to prepare a large part of the decisions required in any society in ways which make them acceptable to all major groups, since they benefit the society as a whole: the building of roads, schools, health institutions and many others fall into this category where adequate balancing of interests is taken into account. Draft decisions negotiated across ethnic groups will not meet a veto unless one of the sides as a matter of principle insists on group preference in all situations. In pure majoritarian systems with only simple majority requirements, the ethnic majority may get away with such a position; in consociational societies with proportional representation and a degree of power-sharing — for example through weighted voting — the majority could do so only at its own peril since it would block decisions that were also important for the voters of the majority group.

Many additional approaches are possible, depending on the size and concerns of the different groups. States participating in a seminar on minority issues held in Geneva in July 1991 by the Conference on Security and Co-operation in Europe, and identified the following positive approaches pursued by European democracies:

- Advisory and decision-making bodies in which minorities are represented, in particular with regard to education, culture and religion.

- Elected bodies and assemblies concerned with national minority affairs.

- Local and autonomous administration, as well as autonomy on a territorial basis, including the existence of consultative, legislative and executive bodies chosen through free and periodic elections.

- Self-administration by a national minority of aspects concerning its identity in situations where autonomy on a territorial basis does not apply.

- Decentralized or local forms of government.

- Encouragement of the establishment of permanent mixed commissions, either inter-State or regional, to facilitate continuing dialogue between the border regions concerned.

4.6.8 THE RIGHT OF MINORITIES TO FORM THEIR OWN ASSOCIATIONS

Minorities must be, and are increasingly allowed to, form their own associations. There are different approaches to this question. In some societies, associations must be registered. If so, States must not limit associations because of their ethnic basis, unless there are acceptable grounds for such limitation.

Political parties, however, based on ethnicity or religion harbour serious risks for democracy, unless there are other parties which can mobilize some support.[38] Voting arrangements or power-sharing systems can reduce the risk of intensified conflict; but it is difficult to find general recipes which are appropriate to all situations. Incentives to cooperation should be sought.

4.6.9 CONTACTS ACROSS BORDERS

Minority members in many States are now fully allowed to have transfrontier contacts and cooperation. States should not, and many do not, prevent persons belonging to a national minority from having free and unimpeded contacts with those citizens of another country with which the minority shares ethnic, religious or linguistic features or a cultural identity. In doing so, however, members of minorities will have to respect the territorial integrity of the State.

Minorities, majorities and outside States, including minority-related States must show *respect for sovereign equality, territorial integrity and political independence for States.*

4.7 DO SPECIAL MEASURES CONSTITUTE DISCRIMINATION?

The protection of minorities requires special measures which might appear to introduce discrimination between individuals belonging to majorities vis à vis minorities. This has to be handled carefully. The 1992 United Nations Declaration on the Rights of Persons Belonging to National or Ethnic, Religious and Linguistic Minorities States in Article 8 para. 2 that 'The exercise of the rights set forth in this Declaration shall not prejudice the enjoyment by all persons of universally recognized human rights and fundamental freedoms.'

All distinctions, however, do not constitute discrimination. To explore this more fully, the concept of discrimination must be further analysed. In international practice discrimination is understood as invidious treatment which introduces unreasonable classifications within the specific context of the rights concerned. There are therefore three elements involved: somebody must be subjected to invidious treatment, it must result from the introduction of a classification, or distinction; that classification must be unreasonable.

The first requirement for a distinction to constitute discrimination is that it leads to invidious treatment. This means that it must be negative for the person concerned. Measures to ensure that minority linguistic groups can use and learn their own language, or have street signs in their language in addition to being in the language of the majority, do not constitute discrimination because there is no invidious treatment of members of the majority involved. In some situations, however, positive treatment of members of one group may have a negative impact on others. Nevertheless, invidious treatment amounts to discrimination only when it introduces unreasonable or unjustified classifications. In addition, the principle of proportionality should be applied: a differentiation should not go beyond what is necessary to achieve the purpose sought and should not be disproportionate to the importance of the goal sought by the differentiation.

The Belgian linguistic case was a leading case dealt with by the European Court of Human Rights.[39] Francophone parents of schoolchildren residing in the Flemish part of Belgium and in the periphery of Brussels claimed that the linguistic system for education in Belgium under the Acts of 1932 and 1963 was incompatible with the European Convention. The Commission had considered that in various respects the legislation was discriminatory under Article 14, taken in conjunction with the right to education under Article 2 of Protocol No. 1. The court found that the exclusion did not constitute discrimination in regard to the children of Francophone parents living in the Flemish part, and was discriminatory only in so far as the Act of 1963 prevented children, solely on the basis of the residence of their parents, from having access to the French language schools in six 'special status' communes on the Brussels periphery. Even this narrow finding of a violation was contested by a sizeable minority.

The court thereby established, in principle, that distinctions made by the law should not be considered to amount to discrimination prohibited under Article 14 unless they lack an objective and reasonable justification. This is not the case if the aim pursued by the law in drawing the distinction is legitimate, and the means employed are not disproportionate to this aim.

In so far as United Nations law is concerned, this has been clarified by the 1992 Minority Declaration, which states in Article 8 para. 3:

> Measures taken by States to ensure the effective enjoyment of the rights set forth in this Declaration shall not *prima facie* be considered contrary to the principle of equality contained in the Universal Declaration of Human Rights.

4.7.1 COLLECTIVE RIGHTS

Do groups have collective rights, or can they have them? Controversy surrounding this issue is due in part to a lack of distinction between different issues involved. At least three aspects need to be examined: (a) are the beneficiaries defined as individuals or groups? (b) under domestic or under international law? (c) if groups are beneficiaries, do they also have a formal standing under applicable procedural law, and who are entitled to represent them?

Under international human rights law, only two sets of rights explicitly mention groups as beneficiaries: the right to self-determination, which, in accordance with common Article 1 of the two United Nations covenants on human rights of 1966, are rights held by 'all peoples', and the right to development, contained in the Declaration on the Right to Development, General Assembly resolution 41/128 of 4 December 1986. Under Article 1, the right to development:

> … is an inalienable human right by virtue of which every human person and *all peoples* are entitled to participate in, contribute to, and enjoy economic, social, cultural and political development, in which all human rights and fundamental freedoms can be fully realized.

While the beneficiaries of these rights, therefore, are 'peoples', there is no further clarification as to who constitute a people, which also influences the procedural problem of standing. As noted in chapter 3, the right to self-determination has been understood to apply, firstly, to the population as a whole in a non-self-governing territory to obtain independent Statehood or join with an existing sovereign State;

secondly, to the population as a whole within a sovereign territory to enjoy democratic government and to continue its independence. In practice, the United Nations Trusteeship Council and the Decolonization Committee have allowed petitioners from the territories to take the floor; this can be seen as an approximation of a status in these matters.

The Committee on Human Rights under the Covenant on Civil and Political Rights has faced this question in connection with claims brought under the Optional Protocol, which affords the only basis for a status under the procedure of that Committee. Article 1 of the Optional Protocol, however, stipulates that communications may be brought by '*individuals* ... who claim to be *victims of violation* of any of the rights set forth in the Covenant'. The Committee's rules of procedure do not provide for group or class actions. While the right of self-determination is a collective right in the Covenant, it can be asserted only by peoples, not by an individual. The Committee has therefore concluded that whether a given group is a 'people' is not an issue for it to address, since it can deal only with submissions from individuals who claim to be victims of a violation of the Covenant.[40] The interpretation of 'people' under the Declaration on the Right to Development is not yet clarified.

In so far as minorities are concerned, the consistent practice in standard-setting activities, at the level of the United Nations, in the Council of Europe, and in the Organization for Security and Co-operation in Europe, is to use the formulation 'persons belonging'. The direct beneficiaries, therefore, are defined as individuals, not groups.

Indirectly, of course, groups are also beneficiaries, since many of the relevant rights can be enjoyed only 'in community with others', and effective enjoyment means that groups have to be involved in their organization. The necessity in many situations to have a Church organization in order to practice one's religion, the necessity to have a cultural association in order to promote and develop the culture are only some examples of this.

There is no requirement or obligation under international law, which prevents States from introducing collective rights in their internal legislation in order to promote group accommodation and minority protection. Some of the rights recognized under international law, while expressed as rights of individuals, can best be implemented if groups are entitled to deal with those rights under national law. Consequently, States may recognize particular groups, allow them to establish their own agencies, and under domestic law deal with those agencies who then act on behalf of the individuals. This is done in many jurisdictions, and there is nothing strange about it.

Some limitations, however, have to be observed. These flow from other aspects of international law: firstly, as discussed above, the rights enjoyed by members of the group must not constitute discrimination against other individuals; this applies also when groups have been recognized as agencies for those rights. Secondly, groups cannot impose obligations on individuals to form part of that group, against their will. International minority legislation generally requires that the issue of belonging to a given group is a question of free choice, and no adverse consequences shall flow from making that choice.[41]

Finally, it should be added that groups cannot impose duties on their members which would be in violation of human rights.

4.8 PLURALISM BY TERRITORIAL SUBDIVISION WITHIN THE SOVEREIGN STATE

Arrangements for pluralism in togetherness are not always sufficient or fully appropriate to achieve peaceful group accommodation. When the different ethnic groups live in separate territorial localities within the State and a great cultural distance exists between the groups, a degree of territorial subdivision of State power and authority can facilitate effective pluralism and confidence-building without destroying the territorial integrity and the essence of political unity of the sovereign State.

Territorial subdivision is not without problems. It can spill over into a process of separation and generate serious stress in the national society, giving rise also to ethnic cleansing and massive violations, sometimes even attracting foreign intervention and causing serious risks to regional security. To find the appropriate territorial solution constitutes one of the most difficult balancing acts in situations of ethnic conflict.

It can also cut across the interests of different elements within a given ethnic group. It often happens that one part of an ethnic group lives compactly together in a region of the State, while great numbers of the same ethnic group live dispersed in the territory as a whole, particularly in the central urban and industrialized areas, and are more or less satisfactorily integrated with the majority of the population. Many have intermarried, and their children have a dual identity which they would like to maintain. Many members of the ethnic minority have found jobs in the larger society. For them, ethnic separation could be a disaster, unless it was achieved in the form of a soft and negotiated autonomy which allowed for participation in the society at large without recrimination. Some of the benefits and problems will be discussed below after an outline of the concept and its various possible contents.

4.8.1 TYPES AND SCOPE OF TERRITORIAL SUBDIVISION

Autonomist demands might fall into several categories depending on the extent of authority devolved to the local group or territory: federalism, constitutionally regulated provincial autonomy, provincial or regional administrative decentralization, and community autonomy.[42]

A federal system is constitutionally regulated and provides the same degree of auto-nomy to each of the units in the federation. A constitutionally regulated provincial autonomy provides a differentiated arrangement where some provinces have more autonomy than others (Spain), or where only one or two autonomies exist while the rest of the State is unitary (Nicaragua, with regard to the indigenous areas on the Atlantic coast). Provincial autonomy is sometimes regulated by ordinary legislation (Denmark's Home Rule Act for Greenland 1978, Finland's Act on the Autonomy of Åland, 1991). Administrative decentralization provides only for administrative, not legislative self-management. Community autonomy leaves it to the community, on a personal not a territorial basis, to regulate its internal concerns within the framework of national legislation.

4.8.2 CULTURAL AUTONOMY

This concept can be used to describe a group's right to teach and use its own language, to practice its religion and to protect traditional values and ways of life from assimilationist pressures ('cultural autonomy'). It corresponds, therefore, to what in the previous chapter was called 'pluralism in togetherness'. It requires that the group has its own institutions which can make decisions in regard to those aspects of its culture, but without a territorial base.

The United Nations Declaration on the Rights of National or Ethnic, Religious and Linguistic Minorities requires implicitly, but not explicitly some limited cultural autonomy for the groups concerned. Laws on cultural autonomy have recently been adopted by a number of countries, such as Hungary[43] and Estonia,[44] in 1993.

The Hungarian law is one of the most far-reaching in this respect. Its Chapter III section 15 states that it is an inalienable collective right of minorities to preserve, cultivate, strengthen and transmit their identity as a minority. Section 16 states that minorities have the right to cultivate their historical traditions and vernacular language, to preserve and increase their national culture, both material and spiritual. In section 17 minorities are given the right to establish social organizations and self-government at national and local level.

The Estonian law, Article 2, states that:

> In terms of the present law the cultural autonomy of national minorities is the right of persons belonging to a national minority to establish cultural self-governments to perform their rights in the field of culture given them by the constitution.

Many governments in Central and Eastern Europe, including the former Union republics of the USSR, have been willing to offer cultural autonomy to groups living compactly together (Armenians in Nagorno-Karabakh, Abkhazians, or the Serbs in Bosnia etc.) but this has not satisfied the groups concerned.

4.8.3 TERRITORIAL SUBDIVISION

This term is used here as a generic term to refer to all forms of local self-government within a sovereign State. The extent of local self-government can range from a minimum (local councils with authority over minor issues within the municipality) to a maximum which comes close to full sovereignty for the units concerned. It can include federalism, autonomy, regional and municipal local government.

4.8.4 DIFFERENCES IN ORIGIN AND EVOLUTION

The origins and present evolution of territorial subdivisions result from two different processes: fusion and fission. Some sovereign States have resulted from a partial union between previously separate political entities ('fusion'); others are going through a process of decentralization ('fission'). Each entails different processes and problems.

Federal systems have often resulted from a process of partial fusion. The units have voluntarily joined together but retained a reserved domain within their territorial unit (Switzerland, United States, Australia). The language used in the US Constitution, the Tenth Amendment, can be used to illustrate this point:

> The powers not delegated to the United States by the Constitution, nor prohibited by it to the States, are reserved to the States respectively, or to the people.

The language is strongly influenced by the theory of the social contract as articulated by John Locke.[45] It is relevant here that the power held by the federal authorities is delegated to them; what is not delegated is reserved to the individual States members of the federation, or to the people.

In the case of Switzerland, linguistic differences are one important factor in the limits set to the processes of unification. Ethnic, religious or linguistic differences had little to do with the federal arrangements adopted for the United States and Australia, and relatively little for the Federal Republic of Germany, though cultural and religious differences played some role.

The inverse process arises when decentralization occurs in what was formerly a unitary State. In such cases, part of the power held by the central government is devolved or delegated, while the remaining part is reserved for the central State. The division of power is sometimes arranged through the use of three lists: one which enumerates the powers delegated or devolved; a second which in more or less general terms enumerates the powers retained by the central authorities, and a third of concurrent powers, where authority can be exercised by both.

Decentralization is often a reaction to past over-centralization, found unacceptable for reasons of bureaucratic overload or for reasons of linguistic or cultural difference.

Competing interests in the field of economics and regarding the role of the State can also influence the quest for decentralization and autonomy. Regional policies of autonomy in Catalonia and the Basque province (Spain), in northern Italy, including the South Tyrol and the Aosta Valley, and in the Flemish part of Belgium are all affected by a desire for lower taxes and a more market-oriented economy, with fewer transfers by the State to welfare purposes in the poorer regions of the countries concerned. It is therefore a mistake to assume that a quest for autonomy is always pursued by the disadvantaged: in many cases, it is the stronger and wealthier part of the society which wants to divest itself of responsibility for the poorer sections.

Examples of federal and autonomy arrangements are examined in chapter 6.

4.8.5 The Democratic Functions of Territorial Subdivision

Territorial subdivision may be effected in ways which make it possible for a compactly settled minority to have greater influence over political, cultural and economic decisions affecting its members. However, it should not serve to give ethnic groups the sense that the local government is exclusively their government. The subdivision should serve only to bring the institutions of power and the service of State closer to them and give them greater influence over it. Decentralization of power and the extension of authority to smaller territorial units can lead to a more homogenous ethnic composition. Very rarely, however, will even the smaller unit be entirely 'pure' in the ethnic sense. The local majority will have to share power with members of other groups living in the same territorial unit. Groups which are minorities in the nation at large can be majoritarian in the region, but they will have to be as pluralistic within the region as the majority has to be in the country at large, if minority rights are to be respected.

By sharing democratic power, the local majority may become more sensitive to the interests of other groups living in the same territorial unit. At that level there will be an ethnic, cultural and possibly linguistic mosaic which must be respected.

Decentralization must therefore be coupled with genuine pluralistic democratic governance in each territorial unit and with the same respect for human rights and minority rights as on the national level. Were this to be safeguarded, the prospects for decentralization are much better, and could help to ease the burden of overgrown central governments without causing fear for groups which are in a minority position within the smaller units.

Decentralization can bring several benefits. To mention but a few, it reduces government overload; facilitates pluralism within the country as a whole by diffusing centres of power; broadens the allocation of prestigious political and administrative functions, and it facilitates the organization of mother-tongue education.

In the transition from authoritarian to democratic rule in Germany and Southern Europe (Spain, Italy, Germany), democratization proceeded together with a peaceful process of decentralization from the extremely centralistic administrations of Franco, Mussolini and Hitler. Until now, the transition from authoritarian rule in the ex-USSR and ex-Yugoslavia, which indeed resulted also in decentralization, has been much more violent and problematic.

An issue particular to European Union law is whether special arrangements made for autonomies are compatible with the 'four freedoms' within the European Union, in particular freedom of movement and of establishment. In Protocol no. 2 of the Act of Accession of Austria, Sweden and Finland, restrictions on the right of establishment, the provisions of services and the holding of real property are imposed on those who do not enjoy regional 'citizenship' (residence rights) in Åland or have not obtained permission from the competent authorities of the Åland Islands.

5. EVOLUTIONARY INTERLINKAGES: INTERNATIONAL LAW, THE SYSTEM OF STATES, AND NATIONALISM

This chapter aims in part to warn against a static approach to group accommodation within States. The international system is continuously undergoing change, and this affects the interests and values underlying group conflicts and their solution.

Having explored contemporary categories of group conflicts and claims in chapter 2, we drew guidelines from international law in chapter 3. This, however, requires caution. International law is still rather weak as a legal system, in some areas not much more than a set of aspirations to how States should behave rather than an effective regulation of their rights and duties. Nevertheless, its significance has increased considerably over time. More importantly for the present purpose, international law is affected by and in turn affects the evolution of the State system; the notion and function of 'State' has in turn been affected by the notion of 'nation' and its various functions, all of which are evolving.

Satisfactory approaches to conflicts arising from competing nationalist aspirations have not yet been found. In the present stage of development in international law, there appears to be a contradiction between territorial integrity and self-determination. Whether this is a real conflict depends on the meaning given to the concept of 'nation'.

There is a paradox in the very concept of international law. It purports to be a law inter nations, but is in fact a law *inter States*. This paradox shall be briefly explored, first by examining some aspects of the evolution which has taken place during the 350 years since international law in our contemporary sense started to take shape, and then by examining some recent trends, particularly in Europe.

International law in our modern sense first evolved in Europe. One common starting point for analysis is the Treaty of Westphalia in 1648, because it has been held to constitute a break with the conception of a 'universal' order, the *res publica christiana,* supposed to be guided by common Christian values as upheld by the Catholic Church. The religious wars in the seventeenth century were also wars about sovereignty versus subordination to an inclusive order. With the Treaty of Westphalia, the beginnings of a State system in Europe starts to take shape, consisting of sovereign entities. The break with the past, however, was not dramatic; it was a gradual process.

5.1 EVOLUTION OF THE CONCEPT AND CONTENT OF STATE

The notion of 'State' and its content have undergone considerable changes. In feudal times, the State was more or less associated with the 'sovereign', in other words, the feudal prince or monarch. The 'State' referred to the apparatus of power and administration controlled by the sovereign. Its territory was the area which at any given time was controlled by the sovereign; through intermarriages or through conquest, territories could be transferred from one sovereign to another. The population were seen as subjects, not as citizens. This feudal-monarchical conception has been shattered by two processes: democracy, and nationalism.

The word nation is interpreted in several different ways. Some use it as synonymous with the population of a State, or even with the State as such, for example in titles such as 'League of Nations', the 'United Nations' and in the terms 'international relations' and 'international law'. Others define nation primarily in ethnic terms, an understanding better conveyed by the compound 'ethno-nation'. The two interpretations have completely different consequences.

It is important, however, to recognize that they also had different historical origins. The evolution of 'State-nation' was affected by the emergence and strengthening of democratic movements within States which were already centralized. The essence of this was not to change borders, but to change the nature of the polity, the relationship between the 'sovereign' and the 'subjects'. In due course, the population which was subject to the authority of the sovereign became the 'people' and the basis of sovereignty. Sovereignty came to be seen as the 'property' of the people, not of the monarch or the feudal lord. This notion of popular sovereignty, which emerged in conjunction with the evolution of parliamentarism, also implied that the word 'nation' was given an inclusive meaning, changed from a reference to a small elite to the whole population.

The philosophical basis of democracy emerged with the theory of social contract, in the way it was reinterpreted in the course of the seventeenth century and further developed in the eighteenth century. It contributed also to the evolution of the concept of nation. In a recent article John Keane[1] has discussed this trend, where the nation is understood as a population of a given territory sharing common laws and political institutions. This is a territorial and political conception of 'nation'. The democratic movements sought to expand participation to involve an increasingly wider sector of the population. The efforts were closely related to the evolution of human rights, articulated and struggled for in the eighteenth century and extended to include political rights for all during a century-long struggle in the ninteenth century. The struggle was directed against privileged classes in society, with anti-aristocratic and anti-monarchic implications. The 'nation' was to embrace everyone, not only the privileged classes; their privileges should be and were abolished, and equality was introduced.

The other trend is ethno-nationalism.[2] This takes the ethnic group as a starting point, defined on the basis of a common culture, language and traditions, and seeks to establish a political unit which corresponds to the ethnic group. The claim is that the territory of that group shall correspond to the habitat of the ethnic group, sometimes with the additional requirement that the habitat which originally belonged to the group shall be restored to it, even if others have subsequently arrived and now constitute the majority. This is the claim of the Serbian side over the territory of Kosovo, which at present has an overwhelming majority of Albanians.

The driving force of ethno-nationalism was and is to defend and develop a common culture. This was held to require political independence, which would provide the appropriate conditions for the defence and promotion of that culture.

Those territories where democracy and nationalism could develop in unison were fortunate; in many parts of the world, that was not the case. When peoples were

93

subjected to alien domination, the possibility of democratic evolution was blocked; in these situations, the struggle for national self-determination easily took precedence over the quest for democracy. It also took different forms, depending in part on the pre-existing relationship between the central authority and the unity or diversity of cultures within the territory controlled by the central authority.

On these grounds Ernest Gellner has argued that there were several time zones in the evolution of nationalism in Europe, and the struggle for self-determination differed greatly in these time zones. In essence, the process was least difficult in Western Europe — with the exception of Ireland. From early modern times or even earlier, there were strong dynastic States in this region:

> The political units based on Lisbon, Madrid, Paris and London, correlated roughly, though of course far from completely, with cultural/religious regions. Come the age of nationalism, and the requirement of cultural homogeneity within any polity, relatively very little redrawing was required.

Ireland, of course, did not fall within the cultural/religious region of London. Nor, in fact, did the Basque Country or Catalonia in regard to Madrid, or the Flemish or Wallonian in regard to Brussels. In all of these cases, significant tension related to territory and self-determination has arisen. In most other cases, nationalist developments were generally more peaceful in Western Europe, and that may be a major reason why there was not in these countries a tradition of differentiation between 'State' and 'nation'.

The second time zone, in Gellner's opinion, was the area of the Holy Roman Empire. This empire contained German- and Italian-speaking populations, or, more precisely, the cultural elites of these areas spoke and wrote German or Italian, respectively. He points out that the two cultures which made up the majority of the inhabitants had been 'well endowed with High Culture, sustained by an extensive literate class ... All that was required by nationalism was to endow the existing High Culture to define a modern nation with its political roof.' These two modern 'nations' arose by the unification of Italy and of Germany from the middle of the nineteenth century onwards, not without wars, but all relatively limited ones.

Further east, Gellner argues, was the third time zone where there were neither well-defined High Culture nor political shells to cover and protect it, but only empires without any national content and patchworks separating social strata as well as distinguishing adjoining territories. In this time zone, therefore, efforts to reconcile culture and policy were much more difficult, arduous and brutal. The area included in particular the Balkans (part of which remained under the Ottoman empire until World War I) and the Austro-Hungarian empire, and the divided Poland.

The tensions over nationalism in these areas, together with great-power involvement, caused World War I. A primary purpose after that war was therefore also to find an appropriate solution to the nationality question. Support was expressed, in particular by the US President Wilson, for the political principle of national self-determination.

At the Paris Peace Conference in 1919-20, however, it was not that simple. Geo-political factors and practical difficulties led to outcomes which did not fully coincide with the quest for a national self-determination where borders were drawn on the basis of ethnic identities. Two problems arose: one, that many minorities were to be found inside the new or reconstituted States; two, severe frustrations emerged within States which had lost territories which included their own ethnic groups. This applied in particular to Germany and Hungary.

The League of Nations sought to establish a system of minority protection based on a number of specific treaties and other undertakings whose implementation was to be supervised by the League, in order to reduce the tensions arising from imperfect applications of the nationality principle. This is how the system of minority treaties first emerged. It did not work well, however. The impossibility of applying the nation-State principle to the 'third time zone', together with the severe inter-war economic depression, led nationalism to become a platform for populist mobilization and to the emergence of authoritarian regimes in several continental European countries, contributing to the dynamics which ended with the outbreak of World War II.

National self-determination in the sense of ethnic nation-States was discredited when World War II was over. The approach taken within the United Nations was therefore a different one: a strong emphasis on territorial integrity, and the promotion of human rights for all. In other words, the concern with democracy within the inherited State was given priority over the division of existing States, even though these might contain several or national groups with ambitions for self-determination.

5.2 DECOLONIZATION

An apparent major exception to the principle of territorial integrity, which emerged during the first two decades of the history of the United Nations was the introduction of the right to self-determination, tailored mainly as a right of the populations of colonial and other non-self-governing territories to govern themselves. This exception, however, made use of the principle of territorial integrity by emphasizing that the right to self-determination belonged to the population and territory as a whole, not to particular ethnic groups — which often straddled different colonial territories.

5.3 IMPACT ON INTERNATIONAL LAW AND RELATIONS

5.3.1 THE TIME OF THE LEAGUE

Democracy and nationalism had their first major impact on international relations at the beginning of this century, eventually with the explosive force which contributed to the outbreak of World War I. At the end of that war, the worst so far in European history, efforts were made to accommodate the principles of national self-determination and democracy in the reorganization of the European system. The principle of national self-determination became important politically, even though it did not yet reach the level of becoming a principle of international law. As noted, some efforts were made during the peace settlement to create States which were congruent with ethnic nations, which sometimes led to partitioning of territories. Nevertheless, for geopolitical reasons as well as practical obstacles, ethnic or linguistic homogeneity could not be fully achieved. As a compensation, a system of minority protection was introduced for some of the new countries and for countries whose borders were extended.

The impact of the imperfectly applied principle of ethno-national self-determination, combined with the encouragement of the ideology underlying the principle, led to profound frustrations both in countries which argued that a part of their own ethnic population had been left outside the borders and by those who challenged the partitioning of their territory. At the same time, governments of countries which now had minorities inside their borders resented the international supervision and protection established by the League of Nations. These frustrations contributed to the outbreak of World War II.

5.3.2 NEW DEPARTURE: THE TIME OF THE UNITED NATIONS

After the devastating second world war, the general sentiment among those who were to structure the new international order was to give priority to territorial integrity over national self-determination. The primary emphasis was on maintaining peace, which was effected by prohibiting the use of force against the territorial integrity and political independence of the existing, recognized States, including also prohibition of intervention. Conversely, distinct non-self-governing territories were held to be entitled to achieve self-government, including independence if they wished.

5.3.3 QUALIFICATION OF SOVEREIGNTY AND TERRITORIAL INTEGRITY: EVOLUTION OF THE HUMAN RIGHTS SYSTEM

By the introduction of human rights as part of international law after World War II, the harshness of the principles of territorial integrity and non-intervention was considerably modified. Sovereignty had to be open, allowing for pluralist manifestations of opinion, religion and preferences, and also allowing for freedom of movement, including the right to leave one's own country and return to it. Similarly, there should be free flow of information across borders. All of this contributed to a significantly modified sovereignty compared with that which had existed in the past.

An additional improvement emerged with the renewal of concern for minority rights, but now in a setting different from that which prevailed after World War I. While the League of Nations had dealt with minorities only in particular countries of Central and Eastern Europe, the present effort is to develop a general system with universal application. The focus is not on those national minorities alone which have a link to neighbouring States, but to promote the possibility for all national, ethnic, religious or linguistic groups to assert and develop their identity. A significant aspect is the emphasis on open borders of States, in recognition of the right to maintain contacts with groups in neighbouring States belonging to the same ethnic, religious or linguistic group.

Thus, we can see a dual development in international law affecting group accommodation: an emphasis on territorial integrity, affecting also the content of the right to self-determination, but with an extended emphasis on the rights and freedoms of individuals under the human rights system, and of groups under the minority system to preserve and to develop their identity, traditions and culture, including language, and to maintain contacts across borders.

One significant aspect of the evolution of the human rights system is that it is applicable to everyone within the jurisdiction of the State concerned on a basis of equality. It applies in general to citizens and non-citizens. To the extent that the human rights system is taken seriously, it significantly reduces the importance of borders and the importance of what was such a hotly contested issue at the beginning of the present century: the political entity to which a given group should belong.

As pointed out above, however, the process is far from completed. Part of the difficulty arises from the fact that democracy and self-determination have both faced different obstacles in different parts of Europe and in the world. The time zones described by Gellner, applied to the European system, give one indication; the three waves of democracy, described by Samuel Huntingdon,[3] provide another explanation of this process.

The content of international law has changed considerably with the profound changes in the State system, and with the substantial increase in the number of States as well as the expansion of the State system to encompass the whole globe after complete decolonization.

The importance of territorial integrity has increased as an essential contribution to preventing aggression and maintaining peace, but peace cannot be maintained without attention to the other side of the coin: the protection of human rights on an equal basis for everyone and the acceptance of cultural diversity in so far as this can be achieved without destroying the common domain.

5.4 THE INTERNATIONAL ENVIRONMENT AND INTERNATIONAL MECHANISMS

Several issues will be very briefly examined here: the roles of and cooperation between 'home State' and 'kin State'; the European 'stability pact' approach, the EU and the 'Maastricht option'; the roles of the Council of Europe, of the OSCE and of the United Nations.

5.4.1 GOOD NEIGHBOURS: THE 'STABILITY PACT' APPROACH

One important preventive strategy to avoid violence is to encourage good neighbourly relations between States, in particular between kin States and home States of minorities. Bilateral treaties containing clauses on protection of minorities can be useful for peaceful group accommodation if they provide a more satisfactory protection of minorities and serve to reduce or prevent tension between the kin State and the home State of the minorities concerned.

In 1993, the European Union took an initiative to this effect, inspired by the then French Prime Minister, Mr Balladur. The idea was to bring together the Central European States that have an option of joining the European Union in the future, and through a bilateral and multilateral process of consultations and negotiations solve their problems concerning borders and minorities. Mr Balladur's proposal was later launched as the Pact on Stability in Europe and was subsequently adopted by the OSCE. The process envisaged both multilateral contacts and bilateral negotiations. As a result of the latter three new agreements on good neighbourly relations were signed during the process: between Lithuania and Poland; between Lithuania and Byelorussia; and between Hungary and Slovakia. The list of agreements and arrangements is open-ended.

The Pact on Stability was signed at the Paris Conference on Stability in Europe 20-21 March 1995. It consists of a declaration of eighteen paragraphs and several annexes including lists of good neighbour and cooperation agreements and arrangements between the interested States and with the member States of the European Union. The projects concern regional transborder cooperation, questions relating to minorities, cultural cooperation, including language training, regional economic cooperation, legal cooperation and administrative training, as well as environmental problems.

Authority to ensure implementation of the Pact on Stability with its list of agreements and arrangements has been transferred to the OSCE, which is to be responsible for evaluating and for monitoring, according to its procedures, the implementation of the agreements and arrangements. It can be a significant instrument in future OSCE activities. The declaration states in para 4:

> Europe is undergoing a period of change and re-organization. Our aim is to direct this evolution towards building a more united Europe based on greater solidarity, open to dialogue and cooperation, favouring, for this purpose, exchanges of all kinds, respectful of national identities and of the shared values of freedom and democracy. To achieve that aim, we shall continue to combat all manifestations of intolerance, and especially of aggressive nationalism, racism, chauvinism, xenophobia and anti-Semitism, as well as discrimination between persons and persecution on religious or ideological grounds. We undertake to combine our efforts to ensure stability in Europe.

The pact relies heavily on the use of bilateral treaties, monitored by a regional organization, regulating good neighbourly relations.

How useful are such treaties? A group of scholars and other experts have studied this subject at the initiative of the Foundation on Inter-Ethnic Relations (the Hague, Netherlands) and at a meeting convened in Vienna in March 1995 they have drawn some conclusions on the subject, including the following:

- Bilateral treaties of this kind are not always helpful but they can be useful as a preventive strategy, provided that both negotiating parties consider that benefits can be derived from improving their political relations or maintaining good relations; that both parties are able and willing to negotiate in good faith on the basis of equality, and that they both have in place basic democratic institutions by which to ensure that the agreements can be effectively implemented in their national law and administration.

- The treaties should contain a general reference to the principles of international law as contained in the United Nations Charter, and a clause to the effect that its contents should not be construed in ways which conflict with international law. The treaty should provide for the establishment of mechanisms at the governmental level for the supervision of the application of the treaty.

- Various possibilities can be taken into consideration, including political consultations and joint commissions. With special reference to the provisions for the protection of minoritics, consultations with the minorities concerned are encouraged. If problems of application or interpretation cannot be solved in the framework of the joint commissions or otherwise at the bilateral level, it is important to secure the involvement of relevant international institutions and mechanisms for conflict prevention, dispute settlement and human rights protection.

- Implementation and monitoring of these treaties would be improved by the widest possible ratification and acceptance by the parties of international human rights instruments and procedures, including adherence to the Protocol to the International Covenant on Civil and Political Rights, opening up the possibility of submitting individual communications, including under ICCPR Article 27, and other instruments and procedures which allow for individual communications or complaints. Bilateral treaties could include commitments to develop and strengthen international mechanisms and procedures including the envisaged new Protocol to the European Convention on Human Rights relating to the cultural rights of members of minorities.

While the Stability Pact was primarily intended for the States in Central and Eastern Europe, it might appear that the approach taken by the Anglo-Irish Agreement of 1985, the Joint Declaration of 1993 and the New Framework for Agreement of 1995 constitute almost perfect examples of such bilateral arrangements which can contribute to facilitating group accommodation.

5.5 THE IMPACT OF THE EUROPEAN UNION ON GROUP ACCOMMODATION WITHIN MEMBER STATES

It has frequently been noted that the 'Maastricht option', through the application of the subsidiarity principle whereby some powers are transferred to the central authorities whereas others are devolved to sub-national authorities, can facilitate decentralization and legitimize transboundary regional cooperation. This facilitates close economic, cultural and other links by minorities and nationalities in the home State with populations in the kin State. Added to this is free movement of labour, investment and trade, all of which facilitates desired linkages far beyond anything that has existed in the more rigid periods of State formation. These options are, to date, mainly available in the European community, but they already existed in regional arrangements such as the Nordic Council and in Benelux. Most ethnically based minorities in Western Europe support the European Union because of these facilities for greater decentralization and transboundary cooperation.

Under the Treaty on European Union, Article 128 (1) has established a Community responsibility not only for respecting the national and regional diversity within the Union, but also for contributing to the flowering of the cultures of the member States. This must be interpreted to mean that the Community must take positive action to facilitate the development of minority cultures and identities. The regional policies of the Community, and the possibilities for local and regional representative organs to participate in Community decision-making, as well as the use of subsidiarity and the notion of Union citizenship contain considerable possibilities for a more flexible approach to group accommodation within States in the European Union area. The European Union therefore may have an ambiguous impact on questions of minorities. On the one hand, it encourages decentralization and regional politics within States, and encourages cultural diversity. On the other hand, the principles of freedom of movement and establishment may run counter to efforts to maintain territorial-cultural identity by way of particular residence requirements and language requirements. On one point, however, the European Union will have a significant positive impact: due to the increasingly close cooperation between all the States members of the European Union, and because of free movement, borders will be of much less significance than they have been in the past. Ultimately, it will therefore be in some future of considerably less significance for the population in Northern Ireland at large whether their territory forms part of the United Kingdom or of the Republic of Ireland. It will certainly be much less significant than it was in the tumultuous years of 1920-22. To some extent, the obligations under European and universal human rights have the same impact, whether a person belongs under this or that jurisdiction, human rights — civil, political, economic, social and cultural — shall be respected for all on a basis of equality.

5.6 EUROPEAN REGIONAL INSTITUTIONS AND THEIR ROLES: THE COUNCIL OF EUROPE AND OSCE

At the regional level, the Council of Europe has developed instruments and policies regarding minority issues as described in chapter 3. The Framework Convention for the Protection of Minorities was adopted by the Council of Ministers in November 1994 (Council of Europe doc. H(94)10). A second instrument called for by the Summit Meeting of the Heads of States in Vienna 1993 is being prepared. This will be an additional protocol containing cultural rights, with particular attention to such rights of persons belonging to cultural minorities. When these instruments are completed and enforced the machinery of the Council of Europe can increasingly be brought into play for the purpose of peaceful group accommodation within the territories of the States members of the Council.

The OSCE[4] has developed significant mechanisms for the prevention of violence in the context of group accommodation. It builds on a comprehensive concept of security, which relates peace, security in the narrow sense, and prosperity directly to the observance of human rights, fundamental freedoms and democratic principles. The interlinkages have been described in the following words by the OSCE High Commissioner for Minorities, Mr Max van der Stoel:

> Violations of human dimension commitments lead to tensions, to societal conflicts and distrust. At times, they may have cross-border consequences, such as involuntary migration. Especially if large groups are affected, the stability of States or even a region may be at risk. In the particular case of minorities, there may be kin-States which feel they should speak up at the international level, sometimes increasing bilateral frictions.[5]

The office of the OSCE High Commissioner on National Minorities was established at the OSCE follow-up meeting in Helsinki 1992. The mandate envisages a twofold role.[6] Conflict prevention is the primary task, but prevention has to take into account the need also for a longer time perspective in search of sustainable solutions. The first step towards prevention is de-escalation of tensions followed by a process of reconciliation of the interests of the parties concerned. The mandate of the High Commissioner is to provide early warning and, as appropriate, early action, at the earliest possible stage in regard to tensions involving national minority issues which have the potential to develop into a conflict within the OSCE area, affecting peace, stability or relations between participating States. It is intended as an instrument of preventive diplomacy. The task is therefore not directly the protection of minorities, but to be an instrument for investigation and resolution of ethnic tension at an early stage. In this task he is nevertheless likely to take guidance from internationally recognized rights of members of minorities, in particular the OSCE Copenhagen document of 1990. During the brief period since the office was established, the High Commissioner has already dealt with a number of situations, significantly contributing to the reduction of tension: the Baltic States, particularly Latvia and Estonia;[7] Slovakia and Hungary;[8] Romania;[9] the former Yugoslav Republic of Macedonia; Albania,[10] and the situation of the Romanies (Gypsies).[11] The OSCE will also have a function, in the future, in monitoring compliance with the bilateral treaties adopted under the European Pact on Stability.

5.7 UNITED NATIONS: THE INSTITUTIONS AND THE STAGES

The 1992 Minority Declaration asserts that the promotion and protection of the rights of persons belonging to minorities contribute to the stability of the States in which they live.[12] The United Nations and regional organizations can increasingly assist in the protection and promotion of the rights of minorities in ways which enhance the political and social stability of the State concerned. This guideline should be followed also by non-governmental organizations.

The office of the United Nations High Commissioner for Human Rights was established by the United Nations General Assembly on 20 December 1993, and Mr Ayala Lasso was appointed as the first High Commissioner. It will be his task, while respecting the sovereignty and territorial integrity of States, to be the United Nations official with principal responsibility for United Nations human rights activity. The issue of group accommodation in the framework of universal human rights will undoubtedly be a central concern.

Article 9 of the 1992 Minority Declaration calls on specialized agencies and other organizations of the United Nations to contribute to the realization of the principles set forth in the Declaration, within their respective fields of competence. Efforts are now under way to plan for such action; a number of recommendations to that effect are contained in the final chapter of this study.

A range of mechanisms and institutions already exist, but their use could be better focused on prevention and to facilitate constructive solutions, inspired by the 1992 Declaration. Several of these will be briefly described below. It needs to be underlined, however, that to date they have had limited impact on situations of group conflict. There is a need to make much more effective use of them, in order to achieve peaceful settlement of conflicts. Better knowledge of the procedures by which they operate, and more transparency in the process of reporting and examination of the reports are also needed. At the United Nations, non-governmental organizations have been given an increasingly significant role in monitoring these processes, providing supplementary or critical information and in disseminating the findings of the relevant treaty bodies. Much more, however, could be done in this field.

Existing treaty bodies operating under international human rights conventions all perform important roles. The Committee on the Elimination of Racial Discrimination (CERD), which also deals with ethnic discrimination could play a key role. It is the main instrument for the preservation of equality within the common domain, the basis for all other solutions to minority situations.

State reports to the Human Rights Committee provide information under Article 27 of the Covenant on Civil and Political Rights on the treatment of minorities. The Committee also receives communications from individuals under the Optional Protocol alleging violations of Article 27. It is therefore in a position to help prevent conflicts which could become serious if they were not addressed at an early stage. Its interpretation of Article 27 might take into account the 1992 declaration.

The Committee on Economic, Social and Cultural Rights already addresses minority issues in its handling of State reports. Apart from reviewing the States' implementation of their general obligation to ensure the enjoyment of the human rights listed in the Covenant without discrimination, specific questions related to minorities are raised, for example under Article 11 (adequate standard of living), questions about guarantees of access to adequate food, to housing and other basic needs for vulnerable or disadvantaged groups, who in many circumstances are members of minorities. Efforts to obtain such information and to remind States of the need to redress situations of unequal access for minorities, are a positive contribution to minority rights promotion. Under Article 13, dealing with the right to education, the Economic, Social and Cultural Rights Committee addresses questions of linguistic facilities, such as availability of teaching in the mother tongue of the students.

On language and education, the role of UNESCO is pre-eminent, including its handling of the Convention Against Discrimination in Education, Article 5 (1)(c) of which emphasizes the right of members of minorities to carry on their own educational activities.

The Committee on the Rights of the Child, the newest treaty body operating at the global level, is also called on to review minority issues: Article 29 (1)(c) of the Convention requires that the education of the child shall be directed, inter alia, towards the development of respect for the child's parents, his or her own cultural identity, language and values, for the national values of the country in which the child is living, the country from which he or she may originate, and for civilizations different from his or her own. When implemented this provision will be a significant contribution to the creation of a spirit of tolerance for pluralism in society. Article 30, which covers children of minorities and of indigenous peoples, corresponds to Article 27 of the Covenant on Civil and Political Rights. In its dialogue with State parties over the implementation of Article 30, the Committee on the Rights of the Child has an additional, constructive role to play in promoting pluralism in togetherness.

Reporting under all of these conventions can have a significant preventive function. There can be constructive dialogue between the committees and the States submitting the reports. Members of the treaty bodies should seek to understand not only the legal situation in the country concerned, but also the nature of the actual or potential conflicts, particularly those related to group tension. They should use their best endeavours to suggest appropriate ways of responding to tensions arising from the coexistence of different groups. Through the examination of reports, the members of the treaty bodies learn about the situations, which can be significant as an early warning about brewing conflicts.

The International Labour Organization deals with issues relating to tribal and indigenous peoples in independent States and performs a valuable role in that regard.

UNICEF has a mandate to protect children. It can use the provisions in the Convention on the Rights of the Child to focus specifically on prevention of discrimination against children of minorities and on improvement of their conditions. UNICEF is preparing a programme to that effect.

6. State Practice: Some Examples

This chapter comments briefly on experiences in countries or territories with divided societies. Before discussing the case studies, however, some general observations are necessary.

6.1 State-Nations and Nation-States

From a State-nation perspective, the territory and the population is taken as given. Ideally, a process could occur to make the population a nation in the sense of considering the State to be its common home. This would not only be the task of government and public officials, it would also be the result of the evolution of a civil society with various kinds of intersecting, non-ethnic and ecumenical groups trying to build bridges across the ethnic, religious or linguistic divides that might exist within the population.

The human rights system, by emphasizing the importance of equal enjoyment of all human rights, is a prime instrument in this process. The concept of 'nation-building' could be appropriate to this endeavour but not all 'nation-building' proceeds in this way. Often, hegemonical groups seek to weld society together through a combination of coercion and persuasion, sometimes combined with discrimination which is counter-productive to forming a harmonious nation.

The State-nation concept should be contrasted with the notion of *nation-State*, which starts from the opposite premise, that a nation, ethnically or culturally defined, shall control the State, and be entitled to use the State for the promotion and advancement of the values and symbols of the hegemonical society. When an ethno-national group finds itself in a minority position within a State, its inclination is to secede or to obtain autonomy in that part of the territory where it is in a majority. Should an ethno-national group obtain control over the State, or over a territory which was part of the State, it might risk pursuing a policy of hegemonical imposition of its values as against the new minority which may have emerged as a consequence of the redrawing of borders.

6.2   PROCESS AND OUTCOMES

In examining the various cases below, it must be recognized that group accommodation is not achieved through one single settlement. Seeking the 'final solution' is usually unfortunate and contributes to a hardening of positions by making it difficult to find common ground. In practice, as can be seen from the following discussion, there are temporary outcomes, provisional arrangements or settlements, which give rise to processes of conflict or cooperation or a combination of both, until such time as a new settlement becomes possible, which hopefully is more satisfactory to the parties, and generates new processes of conflict and cooperation until yet another settlement becomes possible. It is inconceivable, in a deeply divided society, that any kind of technical recommendation can at one stroke eliminate the problems. Temporary arrangements, which are filled with less tension than the previous arrangements, may be achieved from time to time, and if these are combined with arrangements advancing constructive cooperation, conditions gradually improve towards a satisfactory, long-lasting arrangement. It is necessary also to remember that external factors can be of great significance.

6.3   SPAIN

The Spanish political Constitution recognizes the right to self-government of the nationalities and regions which make up the Spanish nation.[1] The territory is divided into seventeen self-governing communities, of which five have their own vernacular languages: Catalonia, Galicia, the Basque Provinces, the Valencian Community and the Balearic Islands; in the last two communities the vernacular languages are derived from Catalan. Under the Spanish Constitution of 1978, Article 137, the State is organized territorially into municipalities, provinces and any autonomous community that may be constituted. All these bodies shall enjoy self-government for the management of their respective interests.

Article 2 of the Constitution reads:

> The constitution is based on the indissoluble unity of the Spanish Nation, the common and indivisible country of all Spaniards; it recognizes and guarantees the right to autonomy of the nationalities and regions of which it is composed, and solidarity among them all.

The Constitution deals in chapter III with the autonomous communities. According to Article 143, para. 1:

> ... in the exercise of the right of self-government recognized in Article 2 of the Constitution, bordering provinces with common history, cultural and economic characteristics, island territories and provinces with historic regional status may accede to self-government and form Autonomous Communities in conformity with the provisions contained in this Title and in the respective statutes.

The Constitution goes on to provide the details about how to establish autonomous units, with the ultimate authority being with the Cortes Generales (Article 144), the Parliament of Spain. Four regions in Spain have been recognized as 'historic' communities, the Basque country, Catalonia, Galicia and Andalusia. The degree of transfer of power to the different autonomies has been a subject of negotiations and judicial decisions in the Spanish constitutional court. The interesting aspect of the Spanish case, possibly a model for other situations, is the existence of a well thought out model for gradual transfer of authority to territorial units who seek it, while retaining an overarching authority by the central government, the constitutional court, and in particular the Cortes Generales.

Spain became a unified State from the fifteenth century on, with established external borders. This was brought about by a monarchial superstructure built upon various pre-union units such as kingdoms, principalities and feudal domains. Extensive self-government continued to exist within different parts of Spain in its feudal form.

This changed in the eighteenth and particularly in the nineteenth centuries, where models of centralized State-nations derived from France and Britain were advocated, but with considerably less impact than in the two countries which provided the model. The difference in economic development also slowed down the process of centralization. Industrialization first developed in Catalonia and in the Basque country. These were already culturally quite distinct from Castile, the politically dominant part of Spain, and through the early part of the twentieth century efforts continued to find a compromise between centralization and regional self-government. The Constitution of the Spanish Second Republic, adopted in 1932, aimed at granting autonomy status to Catalonia, the Basque country and Galicia.

Several coinciding conflicts — tensions between the Church and the secular society, the social issues and the ethno-territorial conflict — resulted in the Spanish Civil War. The victor in that cruel war was General Franco, at the head of a profoundly reactionary political grouping, with an agenda of drastic centralization of Spain. The Franco regime repressed the publication of newspapers or books in Spanish languages other than Castilian, and banned institutions of self-government as well as teaching and news in the other Spanish languages such as Catalan, Basque and Galician.

Opposition to Franco emerged over the years on social, anti-clerical and anti-centralizing grounds. After the death of Franco, Spain managed an exemplary transition to democracy. One aspect of the transition was reflected in the 1978 Constitution. It combined two basic ideas: on the one hand, the notion of a common Spanish State-nation, but on the other, the concept of Spain as a combination of diverse peoples, nations and regions. In this case, better perhaps than in most other situations, we have a model in which there are nations on two levels: the overarching, common nation of all people living inside the territory of Spain, and the notion of separate nations having extensive self-government in their particular regions.

There are other interesting aspects of the Spanish case. One essential feature is the deliberate asymmetry in the political structure chosen. It is not a traditional federal State, because the different units have different degrees of self-government. This stems from the fact that there is not the same need felt in all parts of Spain for extensive self-government, and the accommodation implies that greater self-government is given to those who most strongly demand it.

A second aspect of the Spanish model is gradualism. All authority inherent in the self-government of the autonomous communities is not transferred at once. Some elements are immediately transferred, others are reserved for the central government, and yet others are negotiable over time, depending on the communities' growing capacity to absorb greater autonomy and on their proven ability to handle self-government in a satisfactory way. This flexibility has been one of the most constructive contributions by the Spanish model to other divided societies.

A further important factor is the role and composition of the *tribunal constitucional*, which is the highest court in Spain. This court has the competence to decide in conflicts of jurisdiction between the central government and the autonomous communities, or between these communities themselves. The composition of the court is influenced by the fact that candidates need a three-fifths majority of both houses of Parliament. Consequently, taking into account the particular Spanish system of proportional representation, no single political party is able to obtain such a majority, and compromises between the government and the opposition will therefore always be necessary on this point. This significantly reduces the possibility that the judges will be politically nominated; it also reduces the likelihood that the centralists within the Spanish State will be able to control the nomination of judges. This is a factor worth taking into account in other deeply divided societies, where the role of the courts is crucial in ensuring equality in protection by the law, and in ensuring the preservation of laws that might have been established to reach appropriate accommodation between major and minor groups in society.

The Spanish Constitution has been particularly useful in reducing tensions in Catalonia and in the Basque Province. Towards the end of the Franco dictatorship and for the periods immediately following, violence did erupt out of frustrated nationalist sentiments; this is now much less frequent and the support for secessionist movements has practically disappeared.

Among the important aspects of the Spanish model is that it gives the autonomies considerable freedom to determine the policies concerning language and culture. As a result, the Catalonian language has had a very strong revival, and most people living in Catalonia are now fully bilingual Castilian/Catalonian. In the Basque country, the Basque language had been much more neglected, and is advancing more slowly; nevertheless, there is a clear increase in the number of people who can speak Basque in addition to Castilian.

6.4 ITALY: SOUTH TYROL

At the time of Italian unification in the middle of the nineteenth century, much of Italy was in the control of various feudal lords, some of them subject to the Austrian Empire. This included the area of Trentino-Alto Adige, which included German-speaking South Tyrol and Italian-speaking Trentino. The area continued to be controlled by Austria until World War I, but with strong irredentist movements in the Trentino area in favour of unification with Italy. Italy joined World War I on the side of the entente powers in return for a promise to acquire the Trentino-Alto Adige area. In the peace settlement after the war, the territory was included in Italy. The predominantly German-speaking population in South Tyrol was antagonistic to the incorporation.

The main point to be taken into account with regard to the South Tyrol question is the gradual process by which autonomy was extended, initially with great reluctance by the Italian Government due, no doubt, to resistance among Italians in the region of Trentino-Alto Adige. Three stages can be discerned: the initial Fascist period of ethnic identity, and a deliberate effort by the Government to alter the demographic balance in favour of the Italians by introducing Italian-dominated industry in the area. The second period saw the drawn-out negotiations between Austria and Italy after World War II, based on the so-called Degasperi-Gruber Agreement, signed in September 1946, a compromise between the quest for self-determination, and the Italian acceptance of cultural autonomy. The use of German in education and for public purposes in the region was accepted, including the use of bilingual topographical names in those townships and localities where the German tongue was prevalent. Italian reluctance, however, was evident in that the province of South Tyrol was combined with the province of Trento, which was almost completely Italian. The population of the whole region of Trentino-Alto Adige was therefore two-thirds Italian. This region was given primary legislative powers, except in a limited area where the provinces including South Tyrol were given primary powers.

During these first two periods, economic and social development favoured the Italians. The next stage started with the adoption of the so-called Package-Agreement of December 1969, which considerably improved the rights of the South Tyrolese. More power was transferred to the provinces, including South Tyrol, and that gave the South Tyrol the power to control its social and economic development. Second, the principle of ethnic proportionality in employment was a major element in the Package, to be applied in all public bodies, including State and semi-State ones. Third, all public officials had to be bilingual, and appointment as well as promotion would require language proficiency to be tested through examination. Fourth, the provinces received substantial control over tax income, up to 90 per cent of taxes raised within the province were to be reserved for the use of the province itself, and in addition, State expenditure was to be provided for housing, roads and schools. With these advanced legislative and administrative powers, South Tyrol in the past twenty five years has undergone a significant positive development. This is also because changes in the economy have benefited the South Tyrol much more than the Italians.

Anthony Alcock[2] has discussed whether South Tyrol can serve as a valid model for other areas of Europe. He explores this under five headings: the overall Italian political system; power-sharing and decision-making in South Tyrol; the system of ethnic proportionality in public employment; the status of the minority language; and the question of self-determination. He deals first with the legislative competences within the framework of the Italian political system. The regions of Italy, and South Tyrol as an autonomous province has more or less regional powers, enjoy two types of legislative competence, primary and secondary. Under primary legislative competence regions may issue laws in regard to those matters laid down in their constitutions as long as they conform to the (national) Constitution and the principles of the legal order of the State, respect international obligations and national interests — these include the protection of local linguistic minorities, and the socio-economic reforms of the republic. Under secondary legislative competence the regions may issue laws in regard to a list of matters within the limits and principles of State laws. The net consequence of this is that regional and provincial legislation require approval by the Italian Government, and since a number of the requirements which have to be fulfilled, such as respect for the socio-economic reforms of the republic or 'national interests', legal disputes and delay can easily arise, and can be utilized by those who oppose the rights of cultural minorities.

In South Tyrol, the German speakers constitute a substantial majority. This could generate the risk that as a result of majority policies the rights of the Italian minority would be severely neglected. However, power-sharing is institutionalized. The provincial government must be composed of representatives of both major ethnic groups, in the ratio of seven South Tyrolese to three Italians. So far, this has functioned well in practice but decisions can be made a simple majority. Thus, the South Tyrolese could easily adopt legislation negatively affecting the Italians. That, in turn, might be found invalid by the Italian Government if it violated national interests, including the protection of the local linguistic group. To prevent this situation arising, a majority of the deputies of the minority ethnic group (the Italians) can demand that the vote in the Tyrol Assembly is done by linguistic groups. If the Bill is adopted despite two-thirds of the linguistic minority group voting against it, that law may be contested before the Constitutional Court, and might be declared invalid. Thus, safeguards are also inbuilt to protect the minority within the autonomous province.

A particular aspect of the South Tyrol situation is the system of proportional public employment. The notion of 'public' employment extends very widely, to all activities run by the State or local authorities. This was introduced to compensate for the legacy of discrimination in earlier periods, when the South Tyrolese were excluded from public employment on the grounds of their limited knowledge of Italian, but also in order to ensure that the South Tyrolese could participate in the administration of their territory without having to compete for jobs against candidates from all over Italy. Thus, there is a dual justification behind proportional employment: from one perspective it may be seen as affirmative action to overcome past discrimination; from another it can possibly be seen as an arrangement to ensure continuation of the cultural and linguistic identity of South Tyrol. It can, however, be seen as discriminatory in giving preference on ethnic grounds to the South Tyrolese over Italians living in the region.

6.5   BELGIUM

In 1830 Belgium became an independent unitary State. The 1932 language legislation prompted a process of decentralization, moving it in the direction of a federal system. In 1962 and 1963 the foundations of territorial subdivision were established, by providing that in monolingual regions a given language, that of the region concerned, has to be used in all affairs of the public authorities, whatever branch of government they belong to. This legislation defined linguistic boundaries and divided the country into four linguistic regions, in an agreement written into the Constitution in 1970: three monolingual regions, French, Dutch and German speaking, and the bilingual Brussels-Capital Region. In the monolingual regions all public affairs should in principle be conducted exclusively in the language of the region concerned. Only in the bilingual Brussels-Capital Region are French and Dutch used on an equal footing. Finally, the legislation allows the inhabitants of the twenty seven communes bordering on a different linguistic region the 'linguistic option' of asking the commune authorities to use a language other than the one of the region in which the commune is situated.

The Belgian institutional system is based on a proportional representation system that depends on the population of each electoral district. The Communities and the Regions are authorities with the same standing as the national authorities.[3]

In 1988 and 1993, further constitutional reforms have been carried out based on community conciliation. With the creation of the Communities and Regions Belgium is no longer a unitary State but has taken steps bringing it almost fully to a federal system, albeit with some unique features. The new entities have the power to adopt legally binding decrees, they have deliberative councils and executive bodies, as well as financial means of their own.

The Belgian case is interesting as an example of a country increasingly separated into several political units on the basis of language. The linguistic struggle has to some extent been associated with social conflict, where the relative economic and political power initially resided with the Francophone grouping, but in recent years it is the Flemish side which has benefited most strongly from structural changes in the economy, and this has increased the tendency towards Flemish separatism.

It is possible that the linguistic issue arose first as a consequence of the French annexation of the territory which is now Belgium from the Austrian Empire, in 1795. France pursued an official assimilationist language policy, making French the language of public life, including education. This changed with the end of the Napoleonic wars, when the Belgian provinces were joined with the Netherlands.

The new government introduced Dutch as an official language in the provinces of East and West Flanders, Antwerp and Limburg, and had plans to introduce the official use of Dutch in the Flemish portion of the province of Brabant.[4] It has been alleged that the resistance of the Francophone elite to this policy of introducing Dutch in the Flemish areas was one of the causes for the revolt in 1830, which resulted in the creation of an independent Belgium, separated from the Netherlands.

Dutch control, however, had not generated a sufficiently strong Flemish linguistic elite to challenge the dominance of the Francophone elite drawn from Flanders, Valonia and in Brussels. It is therefore against this Francophone-dominant elite that the Flemish movement emerged almost immediately when Belgium gained independence in 1830, and which has increasingly advanced the claim to linguistic division of the country.

In 1961 and 1963 language laws were passed which fixed the language frontier. There were comprehensive constitutional revisions in 1970, in 1980-81 and in 1988. The outcome was an exceedingly complex constitutional arrangement, by which Belgium is divided into nine provinces and into four linguistic regions (the French language region, the Dutch language region, the bilingual region of Brussels-Capital, and the German language region). Every commune in Belgium belongs to one of these linguistic regions. With the exception of the bilingual region of Brussels-Capital, every commune is monolingual.

Belgium is also divided into three communities: French, Flemish and German-speaking. The communities, which are based on languages, each have a council and an executive. The community councils regulate cultural matters. More importantly, they also regulate education, with some exceptions. The three communities are each authorized to regulate international cultural cooperation.

The linguistic division has implied a profound division within public institutions in Belgium. Almost every major institution in Belgian society is now either split into Flemish and Francophone versions or, at best, consists of a loose confederation of the two groups. This affects political parties, trade unions and employers' associations, but also government departments, even the court system. It is often argued that what holds Belgium together is the bilingual region of Brussels, the powerful capital of the country, which cannot be divided on linguistic grounds.

6.6 FINLAND

This provides an interesting example with a number of useful models of group accommodation. It has two official national languages: Finnish and Swedish. The total population of Finland is about five million, of whom 4.6 have Finnish as their mother tongue, whereas nearly 300,000 or 6 per cent speak Swedish. Finland was part of Sweden for 600 years, until 1809. During this period, the educated class became predominantly Swedish-speaking, and Swedish was the language used in higher education, the administrative authorities and the courts. During the Napoleonic wars, Russia occupied and annexed Finland in 1809. It remained under Russian control until 1917. Russia did not try to russify the population, and Swedish continued to be the administrative language. A gradual change took place during the second part of the nineteenth century, and by the beginning of the twentieth century Finnish had developed into the first language in government and the administration of justice. When Finland became independent in 1917, Finnish and Swedish were made national languages of the Republic. Section 14 of the Constitution Act reads as follows:

> Finnish and Swedish are the national languages of the Republic.
>
> The rights of Finnish citizens to use their own language, Finnish or Swedish, as parties before courts of law and administrative authorities, and to obtain from them documents in these languages, shall be guaranteed by law, so as to provide for the rights of the Finnish-speaking and the Swedish-speaking populations in accordance with the principle of equality.
>
> The cultural and economic needs of the Finnish-speaking and Swedish-speaking populations shall be met by the State according to the principle of equality.

This dual language policy has been maintained without much conflict. It is carried through in all aspects of life. Both Finnish and Swedish are used in Parliament, and detailed provisions exist concerning the duty of government officials and civil servants to know and to use the two languages. For practical reasons, since the Swedish-speaking group is concentrated in certain areas of the country, the linguistic compromise found has made use of personal and territorial principles.

The personal principle means that every Finnish citizen always has the right to use his own language, Finnish or Swedish, as a party before the courts and the administrative authorities. The right of a Finnish citizen to receive service in his/her own language in other matters depends on the linguistic character of the district in which he or she lives. This depends on the municipality, which can be monolingual or bilingual. Under the Language Act, a municipality is unilingual if the minority which speaks the other national language does not exceed 8 per cent of the population of the municipality, or 3,000 persons. Civil servants, for whom a higher university degree is required, need to have a complete command of the majority language in the district where they work, and in the central administration they need also to know Finnish.

The language of instruction is Finnish or Swedish, depending on the pupil's mother tongue. There are Swedish-language secondary and vocational schools and even a Swedish-language university in Finland, the Åbo Akademi University. Finland also has a comprehensive legislation on the use of both languages in street names and in toponyms. The process has led to a high degree of sophistication in accommodating the identities of the majority and minority groups, and could thus provide lessons in the very practical sense of specific arrangements that could be adopted in other divided societies.

One particular aspect of the Finnish case is worth briefly mentioning: the autonomy of the Åland Islands. At the time of independence, the Åland Islands, which had been annexed by Russia as part of Finland, had a population which was almost completely monolingual in Swedish. Initially, the Åland Islands wanted to secede from Finland at the time of independence and to integrate with Sweden. Finland protested, and the matter was taken to the League of Nations, which after some debate decided to oppose the act of secession, but recommended an arrangement for autonomy which had been proposed by Finland. Consequently, the Åland Islands have enjoyed a very high level of autonomy from the 1920s until today, as a monolingual Swedish-speaking area within the sovereignty of Finland, but with very extensive local self-government and with separate participation in the inter-governmental Nordic Council.

The special autonomy status was set up under guarantees by the League of Nations. It has functioned smoothly since its establishment in 1921. Elaborate provisions on the distribution of power between the State (Finland) and the autonomy area have been made in the successive Acts on the Autonomy of Åland, revised several times, most recently by law adopted by the Finnish Parliament on 16 August 1991.

The official language of the province of Åland is Swedish. The legislative body is the 'Lagting', the provincial parliament, elected by all who have a right of domicile in the Åland Islands. The scope of legislative authority is set out in the Autonomy Act, and covers education and culture, health and medical services, social welfare, the promotion of industry and trade, local district administration and public order and security.

The executive branch of the autonomous government is called 'Landsskapstyrelsen'. The autonomous area has its own administrative court, but the other courts form part of the judicial hierarchy with the Finnish Supreme Court at the apex.

The right of domicile is acquired by birth if one of the child's parents has a right of domicile, or it can be acquired after five years of continuous residence provided the applicant can prove proficiency in Swedish. The right of domicile is required not only to vote and be elected for the Lagting, but also to own and hold real estate and carry out business in Åland.[5]

6.7 GREENLAND

Unter the Greenland Home Rule Act,[6] adopted by the Danish Parliament on 29 November 1978, Home Rule Authorities were set up in Greenland comprising a legislature and an executive. The majority of Greenlanders are Inuits, but there are also inhabitants of Danish and other origins. They are all subject to the Home Rule Authority.

The Home Rule Act envisages transfer only of legislative and executive power from Danish to Greenlandic Home Rule Authorities; the administration of justice and constitutional rights remain under Danish sovereign authority. Complete legislative authority is not transferred; fundamental principles regarding the law of persons, family law, inheritance law and the law of contracts remain under Danish legislative authority.

The pragmatic approach is particularly interesting. The Home Rule Act envisages a gradual transfer of authority of legislative and executive power, depending on the increasing capacity of the Home Rule Authorities to carry out the functions envisaged. The fields in which jurisdiction can be transferred are listed in a Schedule annexed to the Home Rule Act; in these areas, the Home Rule Authorities have the option and the right to decide that authority shall be transferred to them. The capacity and the expenses involved determine the extent to which this shall be done; it should be noted that Greenland depends on substantial transfer of financial resources from Denmark in order to carry out the tasks required.

The main official language is Greenlandic, an Inuit language.

The transfer of authority by Denmark to Greenland is on a territorial basis. This means that the people of Greenland as a whole, whether Inuits (who constitute the majority) or those of Danish or other ethnic origins, are all subject to the Home Rule Authority; in the field of human rights, everyone is subject to and benefits from the constitutional rights applicable to all Danish citizens, whether they live in Greenland, the Faroes or in Denmark proper.

6.8   CANADA

The Canadian experience could be examined from several perspectives. In this brief note only one aspect will be mentioned: the significance for ethnic relations of the Charter of Rights, introduced with the patriation of the Constitution in 1982.

Effective protection of human rights is particularly significant in divided societies, but also particularly difficult. If equal enjoyment of human rights in their entirety — civil, political, economic, social and cultural — were ensured with full impartiality, the controversial issues relating to conflicting identities could be handled peacefully. Even within societies which are normally devoted to the rule of law and individual rights, nationalist or ethnic tension may lead to violence and counter-violence where the law enforcement agencies are tempted to resort to stark measures — and thereby escalate the conflict. They may become part of the problem rather than a solution to it. Such processes can be seen in many parts of the world. One way of counteracting this is to have an effectively administered bill of rights which ensures that even law enforcement agencies do not resort to unacceptable types of action.

In large parts of Europe, international human rights are now part of the law of the land. This is not so in common law countries, which still adhere to the principle of duality and have not incorporated international human rights law into their domestic legal system. The United Kingdom is one such example, as evidenced for example in the case of *Reg v Secretary of State for the Home Department, ex parte Brind*, (1991) 1 AC 696 (HL), where it was stated that the European Convention for the Protection of Human Rights and Fundamental Freedoms is not part of English domestic law.

An alternative to domestic application by the courts of international human rights law is to adopt a bill of rights. There has been considerable scepticism about this within some traditional common law countries. One argument has been that common law itself is peculiarly apt for dealing with human rights, because it is predicated upon the individual and her or his rights.

It appears, nevertheless, that common law is not well adapted to deal with the human rights problems arising from nationalist or ethnic tensions. This is one among various reasons why several countries which have a common law system at their base, have introduced a bill of rights into their legal system. I shall here briefly mention and review the experience of Canada in this regard.

In the late 1960s and through the 1970s, the nationalist tension caused by secessionist demands within Quebec started to take a violent turn. Bombings started in 1963 and continued sporadically. In 1970 the Minister for Labour in Quebec was murdered. The Federal Government introduced the War Measures Act, sent forces into Quebec, and arrested 500 people. This situation could have worsened but fortunately did not.

One significant contribution to reducing the violent aspects of the tension was the introduction, in 1968, of the Official Language Bill and its follow-up which prepared the way for a bilingual federal civil service and for the encouragement of French language and culture in Canada. Much more important, however, was the so-called patriation of the Constitution in 1982, with the Charter of Rights attached to it.

This has not stopped the nationalist debate and nationalist politics, which was not its purpose, but it has made it possible to conduct the political processes peacefully in regard to issues whose content is dramatic and which in most other societies would have been likely to lead to open violence.

The Charter made ownership of rights much more effective for all Canadian citizens, regardless not only of gender and race but also of ethnic origin, cultural background or place of birth.

Evaluation of the impact of the Canadian Charter of Rights has shown, inter alia, that it has served to increase significantly due process and rule of law. In particular, it has had a constraining effect on the law enforcement activities of the police. This applies, in particular, to conditions for detaining a person, including the obligation on the police prior to any questioning to advise the detainee of the rights to counsel and to provide her or him with reasonable opportunities for exercising that right.[7]

These and other aspects indicate that a bill of rights can have a useful function, even within societies with competing concepts of national identity, in preventing political conflicts escalating into violence. Much depends, of course, on the composition of the courts and the culture of the judiciary as well as the law enforcement agencies. The framework established by a bill of rights, however, can have a considerable impact on both.

N O T E S

E X E C U T I V E   S U M M A R Y

1.   *The Two Irelands — the Problem of the Double Minority*, London: Minority Rights Group Report no. 2, 1971, p. 4.

C H A P T E R   O N E — T E R R I T O R I A L   D I S P U T E S

1.   Such policies can be observed in some countries after independence from colonial rule, and in more recent times in the countries which have become independent or regained independence following the dissolution of the USSR and Yugoslavia. In regard to the latter, the issue is discussed, e.g., in Müllerson, Rein, 'The Continuity and Succession of States, with Reference to the Former USSR and Yugoslavia', *The International and Comparative Law Quarterly*, vol.42 (1993) pp.473-93.

2.   This is the approach used, in particular, by Serbs in Bosnia-Herzegovina in order to force Muslims to leave those parts of the territory which Bosnian Serbs want to attach to their 'Greater Serbia'. It has been used, though to a lesser extent, in several other recent ethnic conflicts.

3.   The negative consequences for the solution of ethnic conflicts of such transfers are discussed in Palley, Claire, 'Population transfers', in Gomien, Donna, (ed.) *Broadening the Frontiers of Human Rights*, Oslo: Scandinavian University Press, 1993, pp. 219-57. Such transfers, their legality and consequences for human rights, are now the subject of a study by Professor Al-Khasawneh for the Sub-Commission on Prevention of Discrimination and Protection of Minorities.

4.   Genocide is defined in Article II of the Convention on the Prevention and Punishment of Genocide, adopted by the UN General Assembly on December 9, 1948, as:

   … any of the following acts committed with intent to destroy, in whole or in part, a national, ethnical, racial or religious group, as such: (a) killing members of the group; (b) causing serious bodily or mental harm to members of the group; (c) deliberately inflicting on the group conditions of life calculated to bring about its physical destruction in whole or in part, (d) imposing measures intended to prevent births within the group, (e) forcibly transferring children of the group to another group.

CHAPTER TWO — GROUP CONFLICTS AND CLAIMS

1. Gurr, Ted, *Minorities at Risk: a Global View of Ethno-political Conflict*, United States Institute of Peace, 1993, p. 18.

CHAPTER THREE — SOVEREIGNTY, TERRITORIAL INTEGRITY AND SELF-DETERMINATION

1. See also Rosas, Allan, 'The Decline of Sovereignty: Legal Perspectives', in Iivonen, Jyrki (ed.), *The Future of the Nation State in Europe*, Cambridge University Press, 1993, pp. 130-158.
2. For highly interesting analyses of the consequences of modernity and its relation to processes of globalization see Giddens, Anthony, *The Consequences of Modernity*, Cambridge, United Kingdom: Polity Press, 1990; and Robertson, Roland, *Globalization; Social Theory and Global Culture*, London: Sage Publications, 1992.
3. United Nations Charter Art. 2.4.
4. See Hannum, Hurst, *Autonomy, Sovereignty, and Self-determination*, Philadelphia, University of Pennsylvania Press, 1991, pp. 214-25.
5. For a survey of these and related matters, see Tremblay, Jean-Francois and Pierre-Gerlier Forest, 'Aboriginal Peoples and Self-Determination', *Studies and Research Collection*, Secretariat aux affaires autochtones, Quebec 1993.
6. Universal Declaration Art. 21 (3).
7. This language describing the prohibited acts is taken from the principle of non-intervention contained in the Declaration on Friendly Relations, 1970 (General Assembly resolution 2625 (XXV))
8. The United Nations convened the second World Conference on Human Rights in Vienna in June 1993, twenty five years after the first World Conference. More than 180 States and hundreds of non-governmental organizations attended. The document was adopted by the assembled governments by consensus, entitled *The Vienna Declaration and Programme of Action*, published by the United Nations Department of Public Information, doc. DPI/1394-39399, August 1993.
9. Meaning the right to self-determination.
10. 'Declaration on the granting of independence to colonial countries and peoples', GA res. 1515 (XV).

11. On this subject see also Crawford, James, *The Creation of States in International Law*, Oxford: Clarendon Press 1979, ch. 14.
12. What is at stake here is the principle of *uti possidetis juris*, which essentially means to maintain or to freeze the territorial status quo as it stands at independence. The principle is well established and has been implicitly upheld by the International Court of Justice in the Burkina Faso/Republic of Mali case, ICJ Re. 1986 p. 554 ff. It was also confirmed by the Arbitration Commission of the Yugoslavia Conference in its Avis no.2, reprinted in International Legal Materials, 1992, p. 1498.
13. In practice, however, it has not been possible in all circumstances to prevent ethnic dismemberment of the administrative regions: The case of Bosnia-Herzegovina is the most tragic example of the inability of the international community to uphold the principle of *uti possidetis juris*; the consequences in terms of violations and ethnic cleansing have sadly demonstrated the desirability of insisting that States not be torn apart.
14. This has unfortunately not prevented some neighbouring States, also after 1945, from in some cases incorporating non-self-governing territories into their State without proper consultation with the population concerned. In these cases it may be argued that there remains a right of the population of the territory to challenge the incorporation and to demand full independence, should they so desire.
15. These situations are discussed in Crawford, James, *op.cit.*, p. 377-85.

CHAPTER FOUR — HUMAN RIGHTS, MINORITIES AND GROUP ACCOMMODATION

1. A collection of universal instruments has been published by the United Nations Centre for Human Rights in 1993 under the title 'Compilation of international instruments, volume I, parts 1 and 2', covering more than 940 pages, UN publication ST/HR/1 /rev.4/vol.1/part 1 and part 2.
2. The Council of Europe published a collection, *Human Rights in International Law* in 1992 which apart from some of the main international instruments contains the regional instruments: those of the Council of Europe itself, of the Organization of American States, the Organization of African Unity and the Conference on Security and Co-operation in Europe.
3. The notion 'international bill of human rights' refers to the founding instruments of human rights at the global level: the Universal Declaration of Human Rights, adopted by the General Assembly of the United Nations in 1948, and the two main international covenants, the Covenant on Economic, Social and Cultural Rights, and the Covenant on Civil and Political Rights, both adopted by the General Assembly in 1966 and which spell out in greater detail the rights and State obligations arising from the Universal Declaration.
4. The texts of these provisions can be found in the compilations mentioned in notes 1 and 2 above.

5. One of the purposes of the United Nations is, under the Charter, Art. 1 para. 3, to achieve international cooperation in promoting and ensuring respect for human rights and for fundamental freedoms without distinction as to race, sex, language or religion.

6. ICCPR, Art. 2 reads in part: 'Each State Party ...undertakes to ensure to all individuals within its territory and subject to its jurisdiction the rights recognized in the present Covenant, without distinction of any kind such as race, colour, sex, language, religion, political or other opinion, national or social origin, property, birth or other status.' ICESCR Art. 2, para. 2 reads in part: 'The States Parties ...undertake to guarantee that the rights enunciated in the present Covenant will be exercised without discrimination of any kind such as race ... etc.'
    Distinction of national origin obviously includes ethnic origin; such distinction would therefore be a violation of international human rights law.

7. It will be seen that most of these situations were already envisaged in the Universal Declaration, Art. 25, para. 1 *in fine*: '... and the right to security in the event of unemployment, sickness, disability, widowhood, old age or other lack of livelihood in circumstances beyond his control.'

8. ICERD has been ratified by the United Kingdom, but not yet by Ireland.

9. The detailed obligations are set out in ICERD Art. 4.

10. ICERD Art. 5.

11. The civil rights envisaged are specified in some detail in ICERD Art. 5 (d).

12. Listed in Art. 5 (e).

13. ICERD Art. 5 (e) (vi).

14. ICERD Art. 5 (f).

15. January 1995: 141 ratification, but not yet Ireland.

16. The following information is derived from the *Global Compilation of National Legislation Against Racial Discrimination* (HR/Pub/90/8), hereinafter referred to as *Global Compilation*.

17. Examples are given in *Global Compilation*, p. 9.

18. Germany, Basic Law Art. 38, quoted in *Global Compilation*, p. 94.

19. 'Conventional law' here means 'law based on international conventions'.

20. Analysis of the scope of Art. 27 can be found, inter alia, in Capotorti, Francesco, *Study of the Rights of Persons Belonging to Ethnic, Religious and Linguistic Minorities* New York: United Nations 1979; reprinted in 1991 as Study Series No. 5 published by the United Nations Centre for Human Rights; in Nowak, Manfred, *U.N. Covenant on Civil and Political Rights, CCPR Commentary*, Strasbourg/Arlington: N.P. Engel Kehl, 1993; Nowak, M. 'The Evolution of Minority Rights in International Law — a Comment', in Brölman, Catherine, et al. (ed.): 'Peoples and Minorities in International Law', Dordrecht/Boston/London: Martinus Nijhoff Publishers 1993; Tomuschat, C., 'Protection of minorities under Article 27 of the international Covenant on Civil and Political Rights' in *Völkerrecht als Rechtsordnung Internationale Gerichtsbarkeit Menschenrechte. Festschrift für Hermann Mosler*, Berlin/Heidelberg/New York: Springer-Verlag, 1983, pp.949-79; Thornberry, P., *International Law and the Rights of Minorities*, Oxford: Oxford University Press: 1991 (which is the most comprehensive work on the subject); Sohn, Louis B.,

'The Rights of Minorities', in Henkin, Louis (ed.): *The International Bill of Rights*, New York: Columbia University Press, 1981.

21. For a review of cases brought before the Human Rights Committee, see Zayas, A.M. de, 'The International Judicial Protection of Peoples and Minorities', in Brölman, Catherine et al. (eds), *op.cit.*, and Alfredsson, G. and A. de Zayas, 'Minority rights: protection by the United Nations', in *Human Rights Law Journal*, vol. 14, no. 1/2, 1993, pp. 1-9.

22. Comprehensive analysis of the background, content and significance of the Declaration is found in Phillips, Alan and Rosas, Allan (eds), *The UN Minority Rights Declaration*, Institute for Human Rights, Åbo Akademi University, 1993.

23. Now OSCE.

24. During the later parts of the Cold War, at the initiative of leading statesmen among whom Willy Brandt took the lead, a standing Conference on Security and Co-operation in Europe (CSCE), basing itself on the Helsinki Final Act of 1975, met at regular intervals. With the end of the Cold War the cooperation intensified, and at the review conference held in Budapest in 1994 it was decided to transform the conference into an organization, the OSCE. Strictly speaking, documents adopted before November 1994 should therefore be called CSCE documents and those later are OSCE documents.

25. See on this subject in particular Bloed, Arie, 'The CSCE and the Protection of National Minorities', in Phillips and Rosas (eds), *op.cit.*; Helgesen, J. E., 'Protecting Minorities in the Conference on Security and Co-operation in Europe', in Rosas, A.L. and Helgesen, J. E. (eds), *The Strength of Diversity*, Nijhoof, Dordrecht, 1992; Helgesen, J.E., 'The Protection of Minorities in the CSCE, a Note on the Helsinki Document 1992', in Packer, John and Kristian Myntti (eds), *The Protection of Ethnic and Linguistic Minorities in Europe*, Institute for Human Rights, Åbo Akademi University, 1993.

26. The text can be found, inter alia, in 'Human Rights in International Law: Basic texts', Council of Europe Press, 1992, pp. 4442-447.

27. The Charter on Regional and Minority Languages is not yet in force, due to lack of sufficient ratification.

28. See further Thornberry, P., *International Law and the Rights of Minorities*, Oxford: Oxford University Press, 1991, part 4, and Thornberry, P., 'The UN Declaration: Background, Analysis and Observations', in Phillips, A. and Rosas, A. (eds.) *op.cit.*

29. Gomien, Donna, *Pluralism and minority access to media*, 1992.

30. On this question, see, for example the contributions to Frowein, J.A. et al. (eds), *Das Minderheitenrecht europeischer Staaten*, vol. 1 (1993) and vol. 2 (forthcoming 1994).

31. Report by Sweden to the United Nations Human Rights Committee, CCPR/C/58/Add.2, paras 285-91.

32. Report by Romania to the United Nations Human Rights Committee, ROMANIA — CCPR/C/58/Add.15, paras 181-85.

33. Report by Spain to the United Nations Human Rights Committee, CCPR/C/58/Add.1 para. 197.

34. See also Horowitz, Donald L., 'Democracy in divided societies', *Journal of Democracy* vol.4, No.4, 1993, pp.36-38.

35. Lijphart, Arent, 'Majority rule versus democracy in deeply divided societies', *Politicon* 4 (2), 1977.

36. See Rupesinghe, Kumar (ed.), *Ethnic Conflict and Human Rights*, Oslo: Norwegian University Press, 1988, p. 44.

37. Young, Crawford, *Ethnic Diversity and Public Policy: An Overview*, Geneva: UNRISD, 1994.

38. On this point see also Horowitz, *Democracy in Divided Societies*, 1993.

39. Judgement of 23 July 1968, European Court of Human Rights, Series A, No. 6.

40. *Lubicon Lake Band v Canada*, UNDOC A/42/40 (1984), para. 32.1; Communication No. 167/1984.

41. In the UN 1992 declaration (Art. 3 para.2) it reads:
    > No disadvantage shall result for any person belonging to a minority as the consequence of the exercise or non-exercise of the rights set forth in this Declaration.

42. See, for example, Mikesell 1991.

43. Act LXXVII of 1993, On the rights of national and ethnic minorities, Budapest 1993.

44. Law on the Cultural Autonomy of National Minorities of the Republic of Estonia, adopted October 1993.

45. Locke *Second Treatise*, 1689 (1970) passim.

CHAPTER FIVE — EVOLUTIONARY INTERLINKAGES: INTERNATIONAL LAW, THE SYSTEMS OF STATES AND NATIONALISM

1. Keane, John, 'Nations, nationalism and citizens in Europe', *International Social Science Journal*, June 1994, no. 140, pp. 169-84.

2. Among the many studies now appearing on the subject, see in particular Connor, Walker, *Ethno-nationalism, the Quest for Understanding*, Princeton: Princeton University Press, 1994.

3. Huntingdon, Samuel, *The Third Wave, Democratization in the Late Twentieth Century*, University of Oklahoma Press, Norman and London, 1993.

4. The CSCE now comprises more than fifty States, including all those States from Vancouver to Vladivostock on the Northern hemisphere which were drawn into the East-West confrontation during the Cold War, including the European neutral States.

5. Intervention by Max van der Stoel at the Human Dimension Meeting of the CSCE, Warsaw 28 September 1993, distributed at the seminar, dealing with the human dimension and conflict prevention.

6. Huber, Konrad, 'Preventing ethnic conflict in the new Europe: the CSCE High Commissioner on National Minorities', in *CSCE Bulletin*, vol. 1, 1993, no. 3, pp. 17-21.

7. CSCE Communication 124 and 125/add 1 (Baltic States) and 192 (Estonia).

8. CSCE Communication no. 122 (Slovakia and Hungary).
9. CSCE Communication no. 253 (Romania).
10. CSCE Communication no. 251 and add.1 (Albania).
11. CSCE Communication No.240 and add.1 (Romanies).
12. Preambular para. 5.

CHAPTER SIX — STATE PRACTICE: SOME EXAMPLES

1. Excerpts from the Constitution and the Autonomy Statute of the Basque country is found in Hannum, *Documents*, p. 144.
2. Alcock, Anthony, 'South Tyrol', in Meall, Hugh (ed.), *Minority Rights in Europe: the Scope for a Transnational Regime*, London: Pinter Publishers, 1994.
3. Belgian report to the Human Rights Committee, CCPR/C/57/Add.3.
4. Moren Covell, 'Belgium, the Invariability of Ethnic Relations', in McGarry, John and O'Leary, Brendan (eds), *The Politics of Ethnic Conflict Regulation*, London: Routledge, 1993, ch. 12.
5. For further details, see Kristian, Myntti, 'National minorities and Minority Legislation in Finland', in Packer, J. and Kristian M. (eds), *op.cit.*
6. The text is found in Hannum, *op.cit.* 1993, p. 212.
7. Cummins, Patrick, 'The Impact of the Canadian Charter of Rights and Freedoms on the Law Enforcement Responsibilities of the Canadian Police', in Chan, Johannes and Yash, Ghai (eds), *The Hong Kong Bill of Rights — A Comparative Perspective*, Hong Kong and Singapore: Butterworths Asia, 1993.

ASBJØRN EIDE is a leading international authority in the field of human rights. He is Director of the Norwegian Institute of Human Rights which is organized as a centre under the Senate of the University of Oslo. He is a long-serving member of the United Nations Sub-Commission on Prevention of Discrimination and Protection of Minorities, an expert body serving the United Nations Commission on Human Rights. As a member of the Sub-Commission, Dr Eide has been entrusted with a number of special tasks, including acting as special rapporteur on peaceful and constructive ways of handling situations involving minorities and since 1995, acting as Chairman of the Sub-Commission's Working Group on Minorities.

He is a former member of the Council of Europe Committee of Experts on Human Rights Education, Information and Research. He has been a member of CSCE (now OSCE) fact-finding missions to Georgia and Armenia/Azerbaijan/Nagorno-Karabakh.

He has published very extensively on a wide range of human rights matters. He has been involved in the organization of, and contributed to, numerous seminars on human rights throughout the world, including the Armand Hammer conferences on Human Rights and Peace. He has lectured on human rights in many countries in Europe, North and South America, Africa and Asia, including several series of lectures at the International Institute of Human Rights in Strasbourg and the University of Oxford.

He is the initiator of a number of international networks of human rights research, information and documentation, including being a founder member and former Vice-President of the Human Rights Documentation System and Coordinator of the

Nordic Committee of Cooperation for Human Rights Research, Information and Education.

Over the period 1970-86, he was a Senior Fellow and the Director of the International Peace Research Institute in Oslo, an institution for post-graduate research in *inter alia*, conflict studies, armament and disarmament. He is also a former Secretary-General of the International Peace Research Association, a worldwide network of researchers in the fields cited above.

He has been Assistant Professor and, later, Associate Professor, in the Faculty of Law in the University of Oslo. He is a member of the editorial board of the *Nordic Journal of Human Rights* and *Nordic Journal of International Law.*